# Reviews are Cool!

Books by Dom Testa

FICTION

*The Comet's Curse*

*The Web of Titan*

*The Cassini Code*

*The Dark Zone*

*Cosmic Storm*

*The Galahad Legacy*

NON-FICTION

*The Mindbender Book, Volume 1*

*The Mindbender Book, Volume 2*

# SMART is COOL!

## Building a Better Student Through Attitude

## Dom Testa

Profound Impact Group

Books may be purchased in quantity by contacting the publisher directly:
Profound Impact Group, Inc.,
PO Box 370567
Denver, CO 80237
info@ProfoundGroup.com

LCCN: 2014902850
ISBN: 978-0-9887900-2-5

Cover art by Nick Zelinger, NZGraphics.com
Book designed by Rebecca Finkel, F+P Graphic Design

First edition
Printed in the United States of America

# CONTENTS

# INTRODUCTION

Dylan's world inverted in the span of ninety days. That's all it took, three months, to flip him from a straight A elementary school student who loved reading, writing, and math, to a young man in middle school who brought home C's, D's, and an incomplete. Dylan morphed so quickly that his parents were at a complete loss to understand what could've happened. Was it the new school? Could it be his new social activities? What about a physical complication, perhaps eyesight or hearing issues?

At first, his parents were hesitant to question him. After all, they reasoned, every kid goes through an adjustment period when making the transition from elementary school to middle school. After six years of sparkling grades and glowing reports from his teachers, this had to be an anomaly. Surely things would settle down and get back to normal. Middle school couldn't be *that* much more difficult, could it?

But now they held another discouraging progress report in their hands, and those sunny days of elementary school were slipping further into the past. Middle school, it seemed, wasn't treating Dylan kindly. So they sat him down and got straight to the point. What's going on? What happened to your love of reading? Why are you suddenly doing so poorly in school, when last year you were at the top of your class?

Dylan never hesitated. He looked his parents square in the eye and said: "I don't want to be a nerd."

**We have a serious problem.** The issue involves education—which is on the radar of most Americans—but this *specific* problem is rarely discussed.

It's an insidious rot that jeopardizes the futures of millions of young adults, often catching them by surprise; they're usually unaware of it until they walk out of high school and get a cold slap in the face from reality. By then it's often too late.

Dylan's parents found it hard to believe that their bright child made such a quick turn, but they're not alone. We're face-to-face with the intentional dumbing down of millions of young people. Yes, intentional. They're sharp kids, they have the ability to not only finish school but to *excel* in school . . . and yet they choose to blow it off.

And why? Because they don't want the perceived "cool kids" to make fun of them. They want to fit in. They want to be accepted. They want to be just as cool. And if they believe that reading, writing, math, and science skills are apt to get them labeled a nerd or a dork, all of the money that we're spending on education is trickling— make that gushing—down the drain.

Don't be fooled by the recent fad of glorifying nerdy behavior, or what some have tagged as "chic geek." That's all it is: a fad, a gag, a way to exploit Americans' obsession with being contrarian, all for the sake of seeming rebellious. But putting on black-framed glasses and calling yourself a geek is one thing; actually doing the work and fully embracing academic achievement is a completely different story for these hipsters who want the chic label without the pedigree. Visit a classroom in an average middle school in America and you'll find teachers who aren't fooled by the posing; the same kids who jump on the chic-geek bandwagon are usually not the kids sporting the grades to back up their claims.

Instead, many young people are concerned about their *real* image, and consequently they respond by crippling their own academic efforts.

The good news is that a solution exists, one that can at least help to mitigate the problem, and we're all qualified and equipped to help. No Ph.D. necessary. What's more, the solution to this problem doesn't involve treating it with insane amounts of money, admittedly a radical idea in the education world. I'd rather spend the money on great teachers and on saving the terrific school programs that are currently being slashed.

I'm the author of books for middle grade and high school students, and a radio host and speaker, so I travel across the country, talking to students, educators, parents, and businesses. Over the years I've helped tens of thousands of students discover their own creative spark during campus visits, workshops, and conferences. Through it all, I've compiled an extensive history of student evolution and—sadly—devolution. This book shines the spotlight on the issue of dumbing down, and includes solutions to help students overcome this toxic phenomenon.

**Throughout the book** I'll sprinkle in a few anecdotes from my own journey through middle school—or junior high, as it was known in my time. Seventh grade was the worst time of my life, and many people feel the same way. The majority of my nerdy exploits in this book are culled from grades seven through nine, arguably the most awkward, confusing time in the life of a young person.

But elements of my nerdity carried over. In high school I was voted "Runner-Up Friendliest Boy." Not "Most Likely to Succeed," or "Class Clown." At the time I didn't even know there was an award for getting along with people. The award I *should* have claimed was Biggest Turn-around Since Middle School. (There's no such award, but play along, please.) In middle school you would have been hard-pressed to find a kid who was more shy than I was. Or a bigger nerd.

The two often go together. But more on that later.

When I rolled into high school, it was a chance for a fresh start, with a new campus, lots of new people from the other feeder schools, and teachers who didn't know me. When you're a classic nerd like me, facing a clean social slate, there have always been three ways you can go:

**1** **You remain faithful to your nerd genes**, and choose to remain a social outcast from the so-called cool crowd.

THE RESULT: Good grades, a better chance at successfully navigating college, and a head-start on a good career. But during your three- or four-year high school stay you'll often be ridiculed as a (pick one) nerd, dork, brain, geek. You'll be generally ignored by the hot girl/boy in your homeroom class, and somehow your acne will seem worse. (Can't explain that last one; it just works out that way somehow.)

**2** **You go the opposite direction,** forsaking the perceived nerdiness of academic excellence, and blowing off your education. You skate through high school, laughing along with those cool kids, ridiculing the NUMBER ONES—even though you *are* a NUMBER ONE at heart—all for the sake of fitting in.

THE RESULT: You might make more friends, but your studies suffer, your grades erode, and, when you look back a few years later, you wonder exactly what you gained from this tactic. Your life's path, especially your career, becomes a little more difficult, the rewards are tougher to come by, and the cool kids who seemed so important for three years of your life aren't even *in* your life anymore.

**3** **You become a closet nerd.** You keep your grades up, you continue to do the work required for your classes—maybe even a little more—and you keep your eye on the prize. But you hide all of this from the social circle. You don't raise your hand in class, you never let anyone catch you reading, and you still hang out with the cool crowd. You might even still poke fun at a NUMBER ONE, just to keep up the illusion, but it probably makes you sick inside because you really *are* a NUMBER ONE. You've simply cloaked it in order to fit in.

THE RESULT: Essentially it's the same result as a NUMBER ONE—grades, college, career—but without the ridicule. You've fooled the cool kids by becoming a Nerd Secret Agent of sorts, navigating within their cool world while still exercising your brain.

**I was a NUMBER THREE.** During my sophomore year of high school I got a job as a disc jockey at a rock radio station. That's a very cool job, even if *you're* not cool—and I certainly was not. Ask anyone. This weekend gig magically gave my social life a boost, and I managed to infiltrate at least part-way into the cool inner circle. But I still kept most of my nerd side invisible.

When I graduated 23rd from a senior class of 520, my friends were stunned. I laughed.

Okay, so it worked out for me; I managed to fool my friends and do most of the cool stuff while secretly holding on to my nerdy side. But, given these options, a few bright kids will choose to be NUMBER ONES, and just suffer the emotional abuse of being labeled a nerd or dork or geek.

Some other sharp kids might manage to sneak their way through school like I did—as a NUMBER THREE—but it's hard work. Plus, it requires a gene for acting that not everyone possesses.

Way too many kids, however, fall victim to the peer pressure and opt to become a NUMBER TWO. The allure of being in the fun crowd is too strong, the negative attitude toward "smart kids" is too vicious, and every kid wants to be accepted and to fit in with the fun crowd. It's tough being an adult and being different; when you're a teenager, it's hell.

This book, and my education foundation, The Big Brain Club, are dedicated to helping out the millions of kids who are pressured into becoming NUMBER TWOS. The goal is to keep them from sacrificing their education—and their best shot at a satisfying and successful life—all for the sake of a few years of trying to be cool. In a way, I'm trying to keep them from a life that's mired in number two, if you get my drift.

**I have three disclaimers.** First, I want to point out that The Big Brain Club is not about straight-A students, nor is it an honor society, although I'm in favor of those.

No, it's all about the pursuit of learning, about embracing education. That's a characteristic that I believe all kids are born with, but often it's squeezed out of them. That big squeeze is applied environmentally and culturally, but the heartbreaking truth is that kids initially *want* to learn. Have you ever read a book to an eager three-year-old? Even if they've heard the story and scanned the colorful pictures a hundred times, they can't get enough. They crawl right into your lap with that book and joyfully shout, "Read to me!"

That same kid, ten years later, might scoff at the idea of ever reading a book. Why? What happened during that ten-year span to knock them off track?

That's what this book is all about: exposing the problem of dumbing down, while also helping young people to become the best version of themselves. It's about removing a vicious cultural roadblock that trips up a kid and smothers her innate love of learning. It's about grooming a young person so that they don't feel the need to repress their natural curiosity in order to be accepted by their peers. In essence, we're aiming to bolster that innate curiosity.

And it's about teaching students that you don't have to choose between being cool and using your brain. Surprise! You can do both!

Another disclaimer involves the foundation of this book. Please don't confuse it with an academic paper. In my opinion plenty of books about "fixing" education approach the issue from a university standpoint, often penned by professors who are about as close to your average middle school student as they are to Neptune. I'm not knocking their work, which I appreciate; I'm simply offering a more grassroots, man-on-the-street viewpoint.

My background—besides the invaluable experience of living the life of a NUMBER THREE—involves working with tens of thousands of students over twenty years, sitting in their classrooms, walking the halls with them, and talking with them at lunchtime.

And finally, if you think this book is a critical jab at teachers, you're dead wrong. I work with teachers on a consistent basis, and I'm so appreciative of the enormous task they've undertaken. It's often a grinding, thankless job. There are some very good teachers, and some who are not so good. But that's true with every occupation, would you agree?

Instead, this book examines a cultural wave that impacts education, and the emphasis is on the students, not the teachers. My focus is on the young people, and what we can do to improve their attitude about learning.

**It won't be politicians who solve our problem;** debating with the school boards won't solve our problem; and it won't be the parents who ultimately solve the problem—although they'll play a significant role.

No, it's going to be the students themselves who step up and turn things around. This book will outline why it can't be done any other way. For years we've tried to either legislate our way out of the crisis, or we've loudly proclaimed that *now* we're going to get serious about teaching the basics. And all the while the students have gone about their business, paying no attention whatsoever to what Washington or the school boards are arguing about. Why should they? Did *you* listen to Washington when you were in seventh grade?

**At the dawn of this new century in America** we've found more blame and more finger-pointing taking place in the arena of education than almost any other endeavor. People love to blame, because it either

(a) takes the focus off of them and puts it somewhere else, or (b) it's easier to do than actually taking action and doing something positive.

When it comes to our nation's woes in the classroom, finger-pointing has become the only method that anyone seems to advocate anymore. In any given debate, or any article/blog post, the problems will be blamed on:

- ✓ The school system
- ✓ The teachers
- ✓ The parents
- ✓ Television
- ✓ Video games
- ✓ Computers and/or social networks
- ✓ School starts too early
- ✓ Class sizes
- ✓ After-school programs
- ✓ Funding

**Take a good look at the list.** Can you spot the glaring omission?

What about the students?

While all of the issues mentioned in the list are legitimate and worthy of attention, someone needs to speak up and hold the students accountable, too. It's their education and their future we're talking about; at some point they have to grab the reins, push the politicians and school boards out of the way, and do the work that the teachers are asking them to do.

What I'm outlining in this book is one specific, yet crucial, component that robs a young mind of its natural desire to learn. This component is the product of social changes, as well as techno-logical changes, but is layered in its complexity. What I'll suggest—in terms of causes and solutions—will not necessarily be a popular position with everyone, and it likely will have its detractors. Yes, other issues are involved in our nation's lower test scores, but it's fair to say that students have more of a stake in the outcomes than we want to admit. It has become too easy to blame someone or something else, rather than tell a teenager that they need to be accountable, too.

I'll do it.

The challenge is enormous, and this book will spell that out. But the solutions are attainable, and I'll point those out as well. Parents, educators, and concerned onlookers will find many observations and ideas that they can relate to, and likely sink their teeth into. The Big Brain Club is on a mission to help young people overcome the peer pressure that they feel to dumb down in order to fit in.

**Now that you've streaked through the introduction,** you're ready for the meat of the mission. Namely, why are we in this predicament, and how do we fix it? How do we keep other bright young people like Dylan from sacrificing their future?

# CHAPTER 1

# RETROSPECTIVE

We all have landmark moments in our lives, when something impacts your world to the extent that it causes you to alter your attitude and/or your behavior. I love to read the case histories of successful entrepreneurs who met someone by chance, struck up a brief conversation, and found that it suddenly took their life in a completely new direction, one that eventually landed them on a Forbes list or culminated in a discovery that changed the world.

For me, a landmark moment occurred at an intersection, minding my own business, waiting for a light to change. I was listening to the radio and likely tapping my fingers on the wheel, when a white pickup truck pulled alongside me on the left, and maneuvered into the turn lane. I caught a brief glimpse of the overly-hairy guy behind the wheel, enough to catch the muscle shirt, the baseball cap, and a halfway-vacant stare. As he eased forward I glanced at the stickers he'd plastered onto the back window of his cab, and chuckled when I noticed both a Denver Broncos sticker *and* an Oakland Raiders sticker. Obviously a tortured soul.

He also sported one of those Calvin stickers, from the classic Calvin and Hobbes comic strip. Only this was one of those now-tired images of sweet, innocent Calvin urinating on a competing pickup truck logo. Obviously a cultured man.

It was the last sticker, however, that made me stop tapping and singing. I stared at it until the light changed and the hairy guy rumbled away, leaving me to realize that things had to change. This one message, with simple black-on-white lettering, plastered haphazardly to the truck's back window, irked me enough that I vowed right there to do whatever it took to combat the ignorant souls who produced it and the irresponsible citizens who decorated their cars with it.

The sticker became my Landmark Moment. It said: **My Kid Beat Up Your Honor Student.**

Yes, we've all seen it a hundred times, but pardon me if I'm not laughing. Smart kids are already overshadowed on campus by just about every other group, and now we have to step on their necks? So it's fine to boast of your kid's state football championship on your car, but if someone touts their child's honor roll status they have to be ridiculed? The honor roll is just about all these kids get for their efforts, but bozos like the guy in the white pickup have to take even that away from them.

Take a step back for a moment. It used to be different. In fact, when you examine the history of this phenomenon you find an interesting twist. Years ago the most revered people on any school campus were the kids who excelled in academics. One of the more popular television shows was The College Bowl, where students from competing schools squared off in what might pass now for a round of Jeopardy. (Not surprisingly, some former college quiz contestants went on to claim some of that game show's cash.) But if you try looking for the show today, you're out of luck. No national network carries anything remotely like it.

And, although you might find it hard to believe, the kids who competed in these shows were considered—shock!—cool. In fact, it only made sense to the kids of that era; excellence wasn't limited to the athletic field or the stage. That's why there were so many academic all-Americans representing their schools at weekend football or basketball games. In that era, you tried your best at everything.

Kids who were academic standouts were lauded, alongside the students who excelled in the athletic arena, or in the field of music. There was a careful balance in our value system, honoring both brains and brawn. These kids existed, and in significant numbers. No, they weren't always angels, but their priorities were straight and the community—including the media—backed them.

What about the other end of the spectrum, the underachievers? Young people who intentionally goofed off, or who blatantly showed contempt for education, were not looked upon favorably. If you were a slacker, society did not cut you much of a break. You were generally portrayed as a loser, and as such you didn't get the fame, the fortune, or the girl.

But along the way, things began to change. The intellectually lazy wore down the system, until eventually it became the brainiacs who were portrayed as losers. Within a few years it was not only considered not-so-cool to be smart, it was tagged with derogatory labels. You were no longer bright; you were a nerd. You were no longer brilliant; you were a dork. You were no longer inquisitive and curious; you were a geek. And I ask you: how many young adults do you know who are completely indifferent to societal pressures?

Let's tell it like it is. Today, in America, to be dumb is cool. To be smart is dorky. And if my kid can throw a touchdown pass then he is infinitely more desirable as offspring than your 4.0 student. Please don't misunderstand this point. I'm a huge sports fan, and I respect the dedication and hard work that a student athlete invests in his or her craft. But we're talking about a healthy balance here, and today we're not even close to that. At some point in history we ceased to honor the young people who chose a different path from the athletic field, and the class valedictorian fell about five levels below the back-up quarterback in terms of esteem. The net result is that today the majority of students feel as if they have to choose between being a successful athlete or a high academic achiever.

Not in your household, you say? Terrific. And congratulations. It's too bad that millions upon millions of other parents don't feel the same way. And those millions of parents are producing tens of millions of kids who are preparing for their lives with the same mindset as mom and/or dad. And here's a news flash for you: they're interacting with your kids on a daily basis. Your child can't stay in your home's protective cocoon for long, and before you know it they'll be subjected to attitudes about education and literacy that are contrary to everything you've worked hard to instill.

Here's an example that might chill you. I'm often invited to schools to participate in writing programs and assemblies; one of my passions is helping young people develop not only a love of reading, but a love of writing, as well. I steadfastly believe that a child who writes well and enjoys reading will be poised for success later in life. While on these campuses, I listen to what students say about school in general, and about books in particular. At a high school in the Denver area a few years ago I was invited to be part of a program called Author Night, where a dozen or so authors came together to host mini-workshops and to encourage the students to explore their creativity. Toward the end of the evening a girl, decked out in her cheerleading outfit, sauntered through the school's atrium with her mother in tow. When the mom asked the young woman if she'd like to stop and look at some of the books, the cheerleader looked me square in the eye and said: "Only dorks read."

That's not the best part. Her mother responded to this comment by laughing, and then hugging her daughter. Mom gave me the universal look that says, "Isn't she just adorable?" Yes, she embraced her daughter for these wise words, and laughed in agreement, empowering the cheerleader to not only continue a life of illiteracy, but to continue the cycle of valuing—and promoting—coolness over intellect.

Our country squabbles over a variety of educational issues, including school vouchers, curricula, class size, and, of course, budgets. They're all valid issues, to be sure, and worthy of our concern. But an equally daunting challenge for parents, teachers, and students lies not within test booklets and government programs, but rather within the mindset of our culture. When young people declare that "only dorks read," we have a legitimate crisis on our hands.

**So it used to be cool to use your brain,** and now it's often not. In less than half a century we went from celebrating Albert Einstein's creative genius (the guy actually was *the* must-have on every important party guest list) to celebrating the incoherent ramblings of a drunk young movie star or pop music idol. With every awards show they scramble to raise the bar on outrageous behavior. We shifted from honoring great feats of scientific accomplishments to raptly focusing on the garbled musings of a manufactured celebrity. We turned our backs on education, and gave our undivided attention and money— lots and lots of money—to microwavable schlock. We have nobody to blame but ourselves, because we let it happen.

And that's an important question to consider: How did this happen? What caused this shift, whereby we now celebrate ignorance and ridicule intellect? If you think about it, it makes no sense whatsoever. How could a country that has always run on high-octane pride and strength now willfully embrace intellectual laziness and—there's no other way to say it—stupidity? It's a question that has gnawed at me for years, provoking irritation as much as anything.

One answer is the simple strategy that various tacticians have adopted throughout history, whether in military campaigns or political movements.

Strength in numbers.

Slowly but surely the underachievers began to coalesce into what might almost pass as a union of sorts. Sociologists will tell you that like-kind will usually gravitate to one another, almost naturally. The most classic example, and one that you'll recognize instantly, involves smokers. As society increasingly vilifies those who light up, they gather together and bond outside during their smoking breaks. The bonding is key here; it becomes an us-against-them mindset. They even develop their own code language. A friend of mine, for instance, who invested hundreds of hours in these smoking groups outside of office buildings over the years, told me about "smirting." I'll decode that for you: it's flirting during your smoking break.

At parties and other social gatherings, scan the room. There's a good chance that the smokers will find each other and stick together.

Now think about that same bonding process in terms of our educational crisis and its history. The intellectually lazy adopted the same tactic, finding each other and developing their own us-against-them clique. They realized that the best shield against society's scorn was to congregate as a pack. You're safe in an environment where no one can judge you because they share your same belief system. If anything, it validates your approach. Hey, other people are just like me!

Except in this case simply gathering together did nothing to quell the cultural bias against them. They had discovered kindred spirits, but they were still scorned and ridiculed. The next step was to take their collective strength and use it to capture the high ground. To that end they eventually began to resort to intimidation. And don't kid yourself that intimidation isn't occurring; thousands of parents reading this paragraph are already nodding. Intimidation soon became standard operating procedure, only this particular form didn't involve pushing, shoving, and threats of violence (although, sadly, that does exist at times). No, this form of intimidation became couched within imagery, perception, and humiliation.

It's all about hipness manipulation, a thinly-veiled job of propaganda. And the primary weapon in the assault?

Laughter.

It's ingenious. Who doesn't like to laugh? Multiple studies have focused on the fact that while humans are the most advanced of the animal species on Earth (we think), we're also the only species that laughs. It affects us in so many ways, and almost always for the good. Medical experts might not be able to fully explain it, but laughter truly is good medicine. And at our deepest moments of despair, laughter can be the catalyst for saving our sanity.

Okay, so not everyone has a fully developed sense of humor, but even the most sober among us at least *wants* to have one. That's the frustration of being on the outside of an inside joke: we want to join in the laughter. We want the high associated with fun.

Conversely, with only a few exceptions (and these are exceptions that the intellectually lazy take advantage of), nobody wants to be laughed *at*. Nobody wants to be the butt of a joke. It's embarrassing, it's painful, and we'll do almost anything to avoid being ridiculed.

Those last eight words are significant. *We'll do almost anything to avoid being ridiculed.* That includes forfeiting our dignity, our values, and our sense of responsibility. It's extremely tough for adults to deal with being ridiculed; with kids, I propose that it's next to impossible.

When you're young, acceptance by your peers is one of the most powerful motivating forces in your decision making. Whatever mental checklist is accessed, "how this will look to my friends" is perched firmly at the top. If your friends ridicule you for something you've done, your adolescent brain pulls out its own yellow highlighter and marks that moment with one objective: Never do that again.

The intellectually lazy are street-smart enough to know how to play this game, and they play it well. Gather numbers, strengthen unity, and ridicule anyone who openly utilizes their brain. The game is to get others to laugh at the expense of the smart kid. Explore the most efficient delivery system in modern propaganda—the television and movie industry—and you'll find countless examples of the onslaught of 'intelligence lampooning.'

**For instance, *The Breakfast Club.*** This personally stings because it's one of my favorite movies, yet I must acknowledge that it has helped to perpetuate and strengthen the despicable tactics on trial here. In this 1980s classic of teen angst and self-exploration it's crystal clear that the guy you want to be is the one who's the biggest slacker. The character played by Judd Nelson is cool beyond compare, he has all the great lines, and he's by far the funniest person in the bunch. He rebels against the authority figure, who is (naturally) a teacher, and who is (naturally) portrayed as the villain. The slacker character in this film even gets the girl, of course. How could she possibly resist him, right? Millions upon millions of young people sat mesmerized by his charm, and walked out of the theater with a new role model. "I want to be that guy. He's cool."

Then there's the smart guy in *The Breakfast Club.* Anthony Michael Hall plays the dorky-looking brain who is not funny, and ridiculously stunted in the social skills department, to the extent that it's almost painful to watch. He has no friends to speak of. Got that, teens of America? No friends! He proceeds to unveil personal problems that compare with any problems from Judd Nelson's slacker, only—pay attention here, teenagers—Hall's problems all stem from *studying too much!* In fact, at the end of the movie we find out that he's so tortured that he wants to kill himself. He admits to his fellow classmates that his crime was getting caught with a gun in his locker.

Just to make sure that we all understood that message, let's repeat it: If you work too hard academically, you'll end up with no friends, no social skills, and you'll want to blow your brains out.

Who needs that when you can skate by, sass the school authorities, get the laughs, be admired by the other guys, and then sleep with the class queen?

Or take the classic film *Animal House*. I laughed just as loudly as anyone when I went to see the now-legendary comedy from John Landis and the crew at National Lampoon. John Belushi cries out, "Seven years of college down the drain," and we not only laugh, but we want to party with this guy for real. For that matter, the entire Delta fraternity oozed cool. Things like the infamous "zero-point-zero" grade point average, the stolen quiz answers, and vomiting on the Dean . . . yes, I admit it, I laughed. Meanwhile, next door at the Omega house, the disciplined, intellectual crowd are vilified as Nazis.

Wait, I know what you're thinking: It's just a movie. In some respects, you're right. Movies and TV are primarily escape vehicles, and, really, how seriously should we take *The Breakfast Club* and *Animal House?* But . . .

But I maintain that movies also reflect many of our dominant attitudes. In these specific cases I believe that they echo a very real climate of intellectual disdain. They're successful because we want to glorify the rebels and see the smart kids vanquished, put in their place, knocked down a few pegs. The intellectually lazy union has capitalized by using laughter as their primary weapon.

Those are two obvious examples. Now try an experiment on your own. Quick, name a television sitcom where the smart folks are not portrayed as socially inept. Having a hard time? Here's why: Because television only knows one way to play the stereotype, that's why. If you're a writer on a TV show, you automatically make the smart kid a dork, every time.

For evidence, here's a quick roll call that reveals how this particular mass medium has pigeonholed intellect through the years:

**Urkel from *Family Matters*:** Gigantic glasses, snorts when he laughs, wears suspenders, and is pretty much the prototype for dork.

**Screech from *Saved By The Bell*:** A show that millions of kids watched after school. It showed every one of those kids that Screech was a socially-inept nerd, one you laughed at in every episode. Kids pay attention to that stuff.

**Carlton from *Fresh Prince*:** Short, smart, ridiculous taste in music, and always tied a sweater around his shoulders. The perfect contrast to the uber-cool Prince, right?

**Leonard and Sheldon from *Big Bang Theory*:** At least they're nerds that people really like. But still, here we go again with the socially-inept smart guys.

**There are dozens more.** Television shows and movies have made a killing by reinforcing a negative stereotype, and the reason it doesn't bother us is because we're supposed to laugh. And I *do* laugh at these characters, so it works.

Listen, I'm not trying to stifle anyone's fun. Anyone who knows me knows that I inherited a pretty good sense of humor and sense of fun from my dad. But the point is that pop culture has spent several decades pummeling kids with one message: Dumb is cool, smart is dorky. If you think kids don't pick up on that message, and then apply it to their own lives, you're crazy.

You could probably find a small handful of extreme exceptions, where the smart guy/girl saves the day, or gets the girl/guy, or gets the last laugh. Hooray. Intellect gets thrown an occasional bone. Unfortunately these few examples are buried beneath an avalanche of pop-culture-garbage, and the damage has been done.

**Occasionally, after I speak to a group of parents or teachers,** one person will come up to tell me about a student who defies the negative stereotype. I smile and offer my congratulations, and then ask a few questions. Here's what I generally find:

Too many times the gifted exception has other characteristics that set her apart from your typical nerd. For instance, at a conference in Chicago I was greeted by a school librarian who told me that one of their most popular students was a boy who was an honor roll candidate, and who had won a regional science fair project.

But wait. Through probing, I discovered that he was a star player on the school's football team. When I asked how many of the students knew about his exploits in the classroom, the librarian admitted "not many."

Believe me, I love to hear these stories. It's refreshing to know that some students pay as much attention to their studies as they do their athletics, or their other extra-curricular activities. These kids are throwbacks, in a sense, to the days when that was the norm. But what propelled this young man to stardom in the hallways had little to do with academics; instead, he fought through the negative stereotype by excelling on the football field. Kudos to him.

So what about the kids who have no interest in athletics? What about the students who merely excel in the classroom? What's their fate in the social atmosphere on their campus?

One of the biggest obstacles to the cause of my non-profit education foundation, The Big Brain Club, is the exception to the rule. Because *some* schools have students who are popular and smart, and because *some* parents don't see the negative backlash against their honor-roll child, they assume that all schools and all students experience a similar attitude. It's not unusual, really; for ages parents have adopted the blind/irrelevant approach to issues. Meaning, 'if it doesn't affect *my* child, either it doesn't exist, or I don't need to worry about it.'

I say: Walk the hallways at the majority of schools in America and see how it really is. See how many of the "cool" kids are scoring well in class. See how many of the so-called popular kids are doing with their math, their language arts, and their history. Talk to any group of kids, and just ask them how important their grades are compared to their social status.

Be prepared for some of the funniest looks you'll ever see.

There are forces at work that conspire to make sure that the majority of those kids will never reach their full potential. While most Americans assume that the answer is "better teachers," or "more testing," or "more money," the truth lies within the students themselves.

And that's where it can get dicey. The Big Brain Club has the audacity to actually challenge the students to reverse the trends of the past few decades, and to step up and take responsibility.

**In the next chapter** we'll look inside the top three forces that prevent young people from making the most of the education that they're offered.

# CHAPTER 2

# THE THREE
# BIG DOWNERS

Dumbing down is a scourge upon our nation. By populating a society with generations of people who have intentionally forsaken education in favor of perceived coolness, we face a bleak—and potentially dangerous—future. And, as the condition escalates, academic results deteriorate further, making it even tougher to overcome the phenomenon.

Through the early years of the 21st century we've managed to keep at least a semblance of balance between intellect and pop culture idiocy. Our entire technological infrastructure is built upon the backs of great women and men who championed the idea of intellect and creative thought. These hard-working brainiacs worked to make a better life for everyone, not just themselves. Old school examples in the 20th century included Edison and Bell and Tesla and Farnsworth. More recent examples feature names like Clarke, Jobs, Gates, and Berners-Lee.

But with momentum moving in the direction of *Dumb Is Cool*, the balance is eroding. Today we have more and more people with no interest in actually providing anything of value, and instead wanting more and more delivered to them. We are definitely a nation of consumers, which is troubling if the pool of providers is dwindling. (*See more* on this in Chapter 6: The Challenge.)

If all of this is true, then why in the world would we allow ourselves to continue down this dead-end road? The answer lies in the three primary forces that encourage a nation to dumb down. I think of them as the Three Big Downers.

- ✓ Shutting Down
- ✓ Passing Down
- ✓ Pulling Down

We didn't, as a nation, all come together and decree that academic excellence should intentionally be shoved aside. Instead, a lethal combination of factors blindly worked together to create chaos in our education system. Some of it was innocent, but some of it most certainly was not.

And, in the process, we've come to take education for granted. When I read Greg Mortenson's *Three Cups of Tea,* my initial reaction was sadness; sadness for how the children of Pakistan yearned for even the *chance* to go to school, an experience that too often in our country is seen as a burden. Oh, what a little bit of perspective can provide.

DOWNER NUMBER ONE:

# Shutting Down

Back in the day, we honored intellectual achievement. Young people felt proud to be part of the Honor Society, businesses frequently rewarded students with good report cards by offering discounts and/or free treats, and schools made a big deal out of their annual valedictorian.

My own history is sprinkled with examples. In middle school—or junior high school, as it was known at the time—my school selected one boy and one girl each month and spotlighted them for their academic and service achievements. Sure, looking back it seems slightly cheesy that I once claimed the Boy of The Month plaque from Jefferson Junior High—and even my picture in the paper!—but it's also a warm memory of the spirit of success that my principal fostered within the student body.

Fast-forward a few years. I lived in a town of about 100,000 people, with only two high schools to serve that population. At the conclusion of every school year, the top 25 graduates from each school were honored at a prestigious ceremony inside the community civic center. Fifty students and their parents were treated to a chicken dinner, speeches from our principals and teachers, as well as various civic leaders, and we garnered coverage in the local newspaper. I still remember squirming within the scratchy confines of my polyester leisure suit, trying to figure out which fork went with what dish.

The point is, we were honored. We weren't being hailed for an athletic championship, but rather for our academic success. The town was proud to showcase its highest achievers in the education system. A few local businesses even sent letters of congratulations along with certificates for free goods and services, all as a way of saying "well done."

Today individual academic honors are disappearing at breakneck speed around the country. In more and more school districts, young people who excel in the classroom are no longer recognized for their achievements. Why? Take a look at the reasoning put forth by one school district in Nashville. In 2004 they eliminated the Honor Roll program in their schools because it might "embarrass" those who didn't make it. In other words, if someone wants to goof off in class and mock education, Nashville's schools must protect their feelings by denying high-achievers any acknowledgment. According to one newspaper account, "a few" parents complained that their children were emotionally damaged by not making the list. Therefore, the school board reasoned, the entire system must come down.

It's happening at schools from coast to coast. I read a complaint from one student who reported that at his high school the valedictorian was voted on. That's right, they still called it valedictorian, but that pesky GPA didn't matter anymore; instead, it became a popularity contest.

For some, apparently, going to school is more about self-esteem than about education.

If the goal of going to school is to get an education . . .

And if schools are rewarded or punished based on the job they do . . .

And if schools are being blistered by a crushing number of negative progress reports . . .

Then why would schools shut down the programs and acclamations that signify a job well done? Not to make it sound like this is a conflict between academics and athletics (it's certainly not), but I've never seen a school banish any signs or parades when their team wins the state championship in basketball. Have you?

The politically-correct climate has had the disastrous effect of penalizing those who work hard and achieve. Working through an ethos of fear and intimidation, schools are increasingly bowing to the ranting of a vocal minority. I work with a significant number of teachers, librarians, and principals. They don't like it one bit, and the majority of them would love to trumpet the successes of their hardest workers. But they're pressured by a movement to treat students like clones. If they can't *all* be valedictorians, then no one can be a valedictorian. And, by extension, one more incentive for a young person to achieve academically is stripped away, leaving a subtle message behind that there's no need to try harder; just fit in with the group.

In other school districts, letter grades have been abolished out of fear of damaging anyone's self-esteem. Somewhere in a box in my basement I've tucked away a single report card from my days in elementary school. It's the one, lonely testament to twelve years of public school, twelve years of sitting up straight, learning multiplication tables, and memorizing state capitals. It registers mostly A's, one B (never could master art class), and a comment about my improving penmanship. It clearly spelled out my strengths and weaknesses, and neither I nor my parents were foggy about my progress.

But welcome to our more "enlightened" age. A friend of mine explained how her daughter's school district had implemented a point system to replace A's, B's, and so forth. When I asked her what had motivated the change, she rolled her eyes and said, "They're trying to spare the feelings of kids who get D's and F's."

Somehow, I suppose, a 1 is less painful than a D. Never mind that 1 = D. And no, that's not an emoticon.

But it gets better. I next heard from the mother of a seven-year-old who had rushed home with a report card of straight M's. Hooray! Straight M's!

Wait . . . what's an M?

Ah, silly person, don't you know that an M means they've "Mastered" the class? Well, you know now. I pressed to find out more, and discovered that the school breaks it down in this manner:

- **M: Mastered.** (My, that sounds impressive!)
- **D: Developing.** (This has nothing to do with their bodies.)
- **S: Satisfactory.** (Which this scale is not.)
- **NI: Needs improvement!** (Well, don't we all!)

If this shift meant *improving* our education system, hallelujah. But instead it's a cop-out, one that ignores the cracks in the system and chooses to concentrate on protecting the self-esteem of a few students. But it doesn't work that way. If you think an F has a stigma, I've got a news flash for you: kids will figure out in about two seconds that an NI is the same thing as a D or F.

This is a not-so-clever dodge by some to deflect attention from the issue of declining student aptitude and redirecting it toward the preservation of feelings. Some of us are more concerned with academic results. If you want to continually amend the grading system from an A to a 4 to an M, you're missing the point. It's not the letter grade; it's the knowledge associated with that grade.

Students aren't fooled by an NI any more than they're fooled by the small percentage of soccer parents who don't want the kids to keep score during a game. Every child on the field knows exactly what the score is, and they know exactly how they're doing with their school work, too. Dressing up a D and calling it a 1 to make it pretty is ridiculous.

We're in a serious struggle today with our education efforts. It's analogous to a house whose foundation is settling and causing major cracks in the walls. Instead of fixing the foundation we're simply slathering a load of spackle over the cracks, and then feigning shock when the cracks reappear. The whole movement deserves not a 1, nor an NI, but a big, red-letter F.

Lord knows my artwork still Needs Improvement, but the reason I can tell you that Lansing is the capital of Michigan and that the square root of 36 is 6 is because a teacher—and a school district—focused on results. Apparently Mrs. Miller had more important things on her mind than sending me home with straight M's and shiny self-esteem.

I'm disappointed that a child who works her tail off in the classroom can't be rewarded with an A. The Big Brain Club is *not* about straight A's nor Honor Rolls, but it *is* about helping young people become the best version of themselves. To me, if they earn an A, I'd like to see the smiles on their faces when they receive it. We punish these young achievers when we take away their reward.

## Passing Down

We say that we need parents to become more involved in their child's education, but few of them participate. Ask middle school teachers how many parents bother to show up for parent/teacher conferences. Making matters worse, when they do show up, too many of these conferences conclude with a parent berating a teacher for one reason or another. Walk a mile in the shoes of a teacher, I say, to truly appreciate what they handle on a daily basis. It would send most of us running screaming.

We can all agree that there are some teachers who do a stellar job, and there are some who don't, just as there are some doctors who are much better than others. The same can be said with cops, accountants, and realtors. However, just as importantly, there are some parents who are involved in their children's education, and others who show no interest whatsoever. Simply dumping a child into a school system and then taking no active role in their progress is one of the most heinous things a parent can do. It's thoughtless and cruel to both the student and the teacher.

It's worse, however, when negative *attitudes* about education are passed down from generation to generation. It's not simply a matter of a parent neglecting to read to their child, or not helping with homework, or showing no interest in the outcome; it's when the child perceives that the parent's own attitude about learning is poisonous that the real trouble begins.

Remember the cheerleader from the previous chapter, the one who announced that only dorks read? It isn't just her ignorant comment that stands out, but also the reaction from dear old Mom.

The mother embraced her little cheerleader and beamed, therefore sending the daughter away with her negative 'tude reinforced and—even worse—*validated* by a parent. Mom has now passed down to her daughter the notion that reading is not only unimportant, it's just not cool.

A few years ago I visited a book store and signed copies of my young adult action/adventure series. A boy who appeared to be about twelve stopped by the table, picked up my book, and began scanning the back cover, checking to see if he might be interested. A moment later his father approached, looking bored and out of his element. The boy held the book out to his dad and asked him about it, to which the dad replied, "I don't know, I hate to read. Get it if you want."

Not, "Hey, that looks interesting, you might enjoy that." No, instead the boy heard, "I hate to read."

The young man set down the book and walked out of the store with his dad, perhaps to never again attempt to break the cycle of illiteracy in his family. In other words, Dad passed down his own disdain for reading, and reinforced an attitude that reading is neither important nor respected.

Parenting is about many things, but we all agree that one of the most important is setting good examples. That's a no-brainer, you'd think, but over and over again parents—whether it's from weariness or just plain ignorance—inflict severe damage upon their children's natural inclination to learn.

*I hate to read. Only dorks read. Hey, I failed a lot! No, you don't have to do your homework tonight.*

Parents too often fail to recognize that their child not only is a bright creature, but also is highly susceptible to parental influence. We talk and talk in this country about the dangers of a parent smoking in front of their kids, and we worry endlessly about the effects of an alcoholic parent on a child, and we launch campaigns to stop cycles of abuse in families. All of these are noble causes, and I support them.

But why do we not see the devastating impact that parents have on education? It's not just their lack of involvement with the schools—we've heard about that for years. It's about their attitude toward education, the message that they openly and proudly broadcast to their offspring. When a parent brags that they "haven't read a book since junior high school," the child is listening. And if it's good enough for Dad, it's good enough for them.

During an informal discussion I had at a meeting of teachers, ranging from elementary through high school, it was suggested that some parents don't want their kids to excel academically because it would embarrass the parent if they had not done well themselves.

It's not a competition. It's not about one person in a family being smarter than any other. It's about each person, regardless of their position, rising to the highest level of their abilities. If a child has an inherent talent in the classroom, I would hope that would be nurtured by all involved, including the parents.

We want to believe that every parent wants the best for their children; we often hear parents say, "I want to give my child everything I couldn't have." I think that's a noble sentiment, but too often it excludes education, the missing ingredient that truly helps the child achieve more in life.

These are overt examples of the phenomenon, granted, but there are many more that are subtle, and just as dangerous, such as:

✓ Failing to attend school functions
✓ Failing to enforce a teacher's assignments
✓ Ignorance and/or apathy regarding children's pop-cultural influences
✓ Neglecting to encourage and reward academic achievement

- ✓ Reinforcing negative stereotypes of intellectual accomplishments
- ✓ Neglecting to discuss the consequences of poor choices

That last point is crucial. I still chuckle when I think of the simple—and yet profound—advice that one parent conveyed on a regular basis. My son, now a grown man, used to spend some time as an adolescent with a friend we'll call Jeffrey. My son told me that whenever Jeffrey's mom would drop them off somewhere, such as a movie theater or the mall, she would invariably leave them with one comment: "Make good choices." Then she'd drive away.

To this day my son says he can hear Jeffrey's mom. She wasn't loud, she wasn't shrill, and she never lectured. Instead she served up a simple reinforcement of solid advice, offered with a smile, encouraging these two rambunctious teenage boys to consider the choices that they would encounter in the next few hours. It might not strike you as being overly effective, but they're three words that, fifteen years later, my son still remembers. It doesn't take a sledgehammer to drive home an important point.

With education, a parent's positive reinforcement makes a sizable difference. Even eliminating the negative associations carries more weight than you can imagine. If we expect our schools to do a good job of preparing students for a challenging future—and inspiring them to achieve more—we should demand the same encouragement in the home.

There have been legislative attempts to coerce parents into participating, which, on the surface, seem fruitless, while underneath just seem sad:

*"West Virginia considered a bill that would yank a parent's drivers license if their child was absent for ten or more days in any given school year."*

*"The state of New York implemented a law whereby chronic absenteeism by students can lead to a visit by the Office of Children and Family Services, and could result in a trip to family court or even the threat of foster care."*

*"After determining that 44 percent of high school students in Atlanta missed ten or more days in a school year, an ordinance was suggested to punish the parents with jail time and fines of $1000. Each additional absence could incur the same punishment."*

We could argue all day about the effectiveness of these or similar government measures, and one could also debate the ethical question of how accountable parents should be for their child's education. In my opinion, there's no question that parents should be responsible enough to ensure that their children are making the most of their opportunities. The point of this discussion, however, is that the problem has become bad enough that school boards and state governments feel the need to turn to the courts for answers. Does this leave any doubt that a significant number of students approach school with a less-than-appreciative attitude? It's an attitude that too often is fostered by the parents.

A negative attitude toward education and literacy, especially one that is reinforced at home, is an awfully hard obstacle for any school district, or any teacher, to overcome.

DOWNER NUMBER THREE:
## Pulling Down

This is the biggie. Overcoming intellectual peer pressure, sometimes referred to as academic bullying, is one of the most daunting challenges for students. Regardless of their location, their background, or their socioeconomic standing, kids feel the pressure to dumb down on a daily basis.

What makes this force so powerful is that it slams into kids on two fronts.

First, there's the glorifying of stupidity. At some point it became fashionable, and even desirable, to play dumb. An argument could be made that young people put more value in being sexy than in being intelligent.

Once again, pop culture reinforces this flawed conclusion. Movies, television, and the music industry sell sex, and strive to convince teenagers that they're much better off with six-pack abs than they are with a brain. Rather than invest in creative ideas and quality writing, producers are content to populate their line-ups with Jersey Shore, Big Brother, anything with the Kardashians, and Skins, to name just a few. And kids buy it. Boy, do they buy it. Suddenly an entire nation of young people believes that it's much better to be hot than to be smart.

The second front that young adults face comes in the form of taunting. Imagine that you're a sensitive middle school student who has just scored an A+ on a paper (or, for schools that forego letter grades, a 4, or whatever they deem to represent outstanding work). Immediately the snickers are heard in the classroom from the trouble-makers, as they toss around their favorite derogatory terms: nerd, dork, geek.

You're not deaf to this, of course, and you learn right away that the school's "cool" kids don't think too much of intellectual achievement. Now you have a choice to make, the same choice that I outlined in the Introduction. Do you put your head down and work, and just take the abuse, knowing that you won't be included in any so-called fun groups? Do you blow off your studies so that you won't be labeled a nerd or a dork any longer? Or do you still try, but quietly, maybe without the enthusiasm that you once showed for school?

Remember what the cheerleader said: Only dorks read. Of course, not every kid cares what a cheerleader thinks of them, but many do, and many will adjust their own habits to conform, to fit in. To be liked. That's paramount, and it's on the minds of students every single day. Because of it, they'll too often allow themselves to be pulled down to the level of the intellectually lazy. They will voluntarily forfeit their futures for the sake of three or four years of fitting in. It's that powerful of an influence.

For years I've visited schools to present writing workshops and assemblies. In the early days I met with individual classrooms, usually no more than 30 students at a time. In the past few years, however, I've been booked for much larger presentations, sometimes as many as 800 or more students, packed into an auditorium or gymnasium.

The large gatherings in the gym allow me to watch the tidal forces at work. In a small classroom setting, it's difficult for the slacker to pull down his classmates through attitude and intimidation. But in the relatively anonymous pack that crowded bleachers provide, it's easy to see them work their magic. I never stand still behind a podium during these sessions, choosing instead to walk back and forth, making eye contact and establishing connections with students.

With the multitude of faces staring back at me, I can spot the snickering few who have one goal in mind during the assembly: lampoon the speaker, and anyone who's invested in listening. And with their muffled comments, you also can observe the effect on the students around them. Teachers and other faculty members do their best to police the situation, but they can't position themselves within every knot of students among hundreds.

Remember, for the disruptive students it's a method of validating their own attitude toward education, a scorecard of sorts to see how many minds they can manipulate into their camp. In a small classroom they're often stifled, but the anonymity of a crowded gym provides perfect cover.

This particular downer also raises its head online. Most people feel practically invisible—and therefore invulnerable—in an online community, a condition that often cultivates negative attitudes. Social networking, while providing a wealth of positive connections and opportunities, also sports a truly nasty side. In particular, the glorification of bad behavior runs amok, while few are brave enough to post anything that trumpets academic success.

The Big Brain Club has its own fan page online, and we use that outlet to share the academic achievements of average students across the country, as well as snapshot stories of well-known individuals who set a good example. It's simply another tool we employ for positive change. The posts and comments from hard-working students is uplifting and inspirational.

But the occasional mean-spirited replies to some of these posts remind us that we have our work cut out for us. Once again hiding behind the veil of the crowd, it's easy for those who mock education to lash out and attempt to deride those who truly care about their futures. While some may argue that the negative behavior is merely to get attention, the results are the same: young people with little ambition doing everything in their power to instill a similar attitude in others. Again, seeking validation.

This third downer—Pulling Down—often has its roots in the first two, in that either it has been encouraged by society's indifference to academic achievement, or it's been backed up by a negative attitude at home. Either way it's heartbreaking.

But it also fortifies us in our mission. Young people with solid goals for themselves, and with the vision and determination to reach those goals, are young people you want to fight for.

**Shutting down,** perpetrated through a culture of being politically correct.

**Passing down,** inflicted upon young people by parents who either can't see the damage they're causing, or who don't care.

**Pulling down,** the merciless march of ignorance that glorifies idiots and mocks anyone with intellectual dreams.

Three big downers. Three forces threatening the futures of countless millions of impressionable students across the country. Each downer creates a daunting strain on the efforts of educators and parents to encourage academic success in America. But they're three reasons why we need to rally in our efforts to educate our kids.

If you're beginning to grasp how serious this problem is, the next chapter should cement the issue. We'll analyze the often-confusing behavior of the students themselves, including faking it, false uniqueness, and their inability to see beyond today.

# CHAPTER 3

# THE ROOT OF THE EVIL

Who, What, When, Where, Why. Journalism students learn the basics of story-telling when they're still in high school, including the simple elements of research. In this case, we know WHAT the problem is, we see WHO it's affecting, and to discover the WHEN and WHERE just look around. *Now* and *everywhere* are the answers.

That leaves us with a gaping WHY. Why is this happening to so many bright students? Why do they allow it to happen? Why do *we* allow it to happen? And why aren't more people doing something about it? If you get the feeling that this is the most passionate chapter in the book, it's because this is where we get to the root of the issue. It fires me up.

It's time to look at the ingredients of the phenomenon. Talk with your average public school educator and you'll likely find that they have seen each of the following elements at play in the classrooms and hallways of their school. You might see your kids for three to four hours a day, but teachers see them for six or seven. They can attest to the following factors:

- ✓ Faking it to fit in
- ✓ False uniqueness
- ✓ Follow the leader
- ✓ Failure to see the future

I didn't originally intend these particular sub-chapters to all begin with the letter F, but upon further consideration I like the intensity they bring in foreshadowing the future. Straight F's.

## Faking it to fit in

We'll change her name to protect her anonymity, and call her Amanda. She's 14 years old, enjoys sports, likes to read, and loves music. Amanda is a typical teenager in many ways, hanging out with friends, talking about school, about boys, and often about celebrities.

What I find interesting, however, is the *real* Amanda whom she disguises in order to fit in with the social circle. When we talked—away from her friends—I discovered that a lot of the music she listened to in front of those friends held no interest for her whatsoever. She also admitted that she claimed to like certain celebrities because—and these are her words—"a lot of kids at school like them."

Yes, Amanda actually pretends to like some music and some celebrities only because her friends do. A couple of these stars are "stupid," she told me. So why, I asked, do you follow them? "They're popular," she said.

Listen, Amanda is not the first teenager who goes along to get along, basing her decisions on the tide of popularity. Often the thinking is: If everyone else likes this, I should, too. Or—even worse—there must be something wrong with me if I don't like it.

For many young adults, this herd mentality will begin to fade by either the late teens or early 20s, when they'll realize that it's not as important to blend in or follow the crowd.

I casually asked Amanda what music *she* enjoyed. She actually seemed embarrassed to admit what she liked, as if it stained her somehow.

**All of this might seem relatively mild,** but there's another, more dastardly issue at work here. Peer pressure is such a stifling, dominating force in the world of young adults, they will sadly live a false life in order to appear like everyone else. Again the irony pops up, where kids *say* they want to be different, and yet they'll sacrifice their own tastes and desires in order to fit in with the crowd.

Style and fashion are two other prominent examples. If it's so important for young people to be "individuals," and to "express themselves," why do they all flock to the same clothing styles, the same hair styles, the same slang, the same . . . everything. Their social network pages have almost identical postings, those that read tend to read the exact same books, and they'll clump together in the same movie theater on the same night. It's not because they're faulty in any way; it's because we are a social, herd-like society. Fitting in is what young people do, because it allows them to be considered part of the tribe. And, it's important to note that this tribe membership is near the top of their priorities.

Now consider their education. In this book's Introduction, I talked about the three courses that a young person can take, and two of those three involve living a lie. They might be incredibly sharp kids, but they'll dumb down because that's the message they get from pop culture, and from many in their peer group. Or, they'll continue to do the work, but will hide their accomplishments. They become closet nerds, afraid to display their talents in the classroom for fear of being ridiculed. They sometimes even fake a disdain of education to fit into a clique with an aura of cool, while inside their chests their nerd hearts still beat just as strong. It's not until they graduate that they realize how ridiculous that perceived sense of cool really is. It takes the wisdom gained from experience, along with basic maturity, to expose the fraud of ignorance.

Both of these paths explain the frustration felt by so many parents and educators. They know these kids, and they know what they're capable of achieving. In many cases they see a student who has excelled for years in the classroom suddenly fall into an abyss of poor grades and lackadaisical study habits. Adults are flummoxed, because it seems that everyone's talking about education's ills, new programs are sprouting up left and right, and billions upon billions of dollars are being invested into the system. You can quadruple the money, and trumpet new programs every week, but if the students are intentionally dumbing down and rejecting education for the sake of image, every penny is wasted.

Don't get me wrong. This is not some insidious plot by kids to wreck the education system. If they thought that being smart was the ticket to being cool, we'd be awash in honor students. But that's not the way it's perceived by millions of young people. And believe me, if they're willing to fake an interest in a pop music performer or a movie star in order to fit in with the crowd, they'll scuttle their own studies in school, too. They want to be accepted more than anything in the world.

I propose that you tell your students the same thing I told Amanda: You're not a sheep. If you think a particular movie is garbage, you don't have to pretend to like it just because your friends do. The same with music. And, most especially, with pop culture "stars." In fact, I would hope you would expect celebrities to earn your respect. Don't join the bandwagon just because others do. Support the artists and entertainers you truly respect and enjoy. You don't owe allegiance to any celebrity.

Likewise, you don't owe allegiance to anyone who doesn't want you to succeed. If you enjoy math and science, be proud of it. If you like to read and write, shrug off anyone who gives you grief. Keep your standards high, but, more importantly, make sure they're *your* standards, not someone else's.

## False uniqueness

Americans take great pride in their individuality. Frank Sinatra hit it big with *My Way* because our culture professes a love for not only individualism, but for the gritty determination it takes to succeed as a lone wolf. We respect someone who carves out a unique position or product, especially if they overcome the odds to win. And since the days of James Dean and Marlon Brando we've put special emphasis on the singular trait that separates the truly unique: rebelliousness. America loves its rebels.

Again, young people are not immune. In fact, they have embraced the attitude and demeanor of the rebel. The problem is that they often confuse outrageous behavior for individuality.

With the explosive combination of online videos and social networking, it's now easier than ever to stand out for a few shining moments. It's tempting for kids to try to raise the bar on outrageous behavior. For one thing, it's easy. It's a shortcut that doesn't require any creative thought or hard work. In their minds, if it worked for that guy, it can work for me.

Every few years you'll find surveys in which young people are asked a simple question: What do you want to be when you grow up? For years the answers revolved around occupations. Firefighter, doctor, astronaut, and teacher were some of the most popular responses. But not anymore. Now the top answers no longer involve a career. According to a Pew Research Center study in 2007, when asked "what do you want to be when you grow up?" the majority of young people said "rich and famous."

Why this shift? I'm convinced it's a result of the combination of pop culture and the explosion of mass communications. That includes the hysteria involving so-called 'reality TV,' along with YouTube and other assorted internet phenomena which distribute pictures and sound to a worldwide audience in seconds. These examples offer a promise of fame (and perhaps fortune) with what seems like a shortcut to the top. The internet offers a potentially huge audience, and thrives on spotlighting 'regular people' who make it big. The prize seems so easy, and so accessible. Every young person in America can go to sleep at night thinking, "I can do that."

But sadly, there's often nothing in these star-making vehicles that requires a person to be good at anything. Countless *American Idol* wannabes have proven that one can become famous by actually showing almost *no* talent. Just do an online search of William Hung. It didn't take long until there was a parade of copycats lining up, doing their best to look and sound their worst, all for the sake of claiming even one minute of national airtime.

Log onto the web and you'll find that some of the most widely-viewed online videos capture people at their worst. It's not a matter of practicing and perfecting; now all you need to do is stand out. And if the surveys are to be believed, that seems to be the only thing that many young people ache for. They practically scream, "Notice me!"

The definition of unique, especially when it pertains to rebels, has become distorted. It's a fake uniqueness, really, because it ignores the fact that too many of these rebels all fall into the same broad category: Attention hounds. It's one thing to be unique because you stand for something, or you possess a talent that dazzles. It's another thing to desperately scramble for attention by being 'outrageous,' and then label yourself unique.

I remember the day that our office was buzzing, and the bandwidth on Facebook was especially taxed in our zip code, because of Bikini Boy. Every hallway greeting at work was punctuated with "Did you see him?" and there was an overdose of the already-crispy LOL abbreviation exchanged between friends. Twenty-five million people in America had stared vacuously at their television screens the night before as a young man paraded across the very-staged stage of American Idol, dressed in a bikini.

This young man, Bikini Boy, worked in our office. It was one of those rare instances where you're actually acquainted with a person who is instantly—albeit briefly—thrust into the American public's consciousness. They're a flashbulb celebrity, shining brightly in front of a large audience before immediately fading back into obscurity, to be replaced by the next morsel demanded by an audience starved for distraction. They're the empty calories of today's entertainment buffet.

We are a nation full of gimmicks, with one hard-and-fast rule: Whatever the ruse, it must be at least 0.5 percent more outrageous than the gimmick you saw an hour ago. And, given the 24-hours of anime-eyed viewers waiting for the next AMAZING/OUTRAGEOUS/AWESOME spectacle to slip past on the conveyor belt . . . well, just how high can the bar be raised? Or lowered, if you think about it.

If you're in a position of influence in the life of a young person, it's important to explain the difference between gimmicks and substance. *You* might know the difference, but their world has adopted a reverence for fluff, to the point where their ambitions might be skewed toward the absurd. The line between gimmicks and real life has not only been blurred, but trampled into invisibility, like the hash-marks on a muddy football field.

Is there harm in an endless diet of gimmickry? I don't know the answer for sure, but I have a strong feeling, just as you probably do. At the very least, a wave of mindless fluff likely acts as a smokescreen, obscuring other messages and lessons that would offer so much more in the long run.

**It's not as if adults haven't been complicit.** For years we've trumpeted those whose thinking went against conventional wisdom. We held in high esteem the ones who zigged while the rest of us were still practicing our zag. The popular vernacular for these contrarians even segregated them from the masses, placing them outside the normal boundaries.

Yes, they think *outside the box.*

But when you elevate the status of anything, especially the perceived reverence of the uber-cool contrarian, you immediately invite everyone into the pool. From far and wide there's a rush to crowd into that VIP box, where one and all are glorified for coloring outside the lines, for bucking the trend, for—yes, let's say it again—thinking outside the box.

Yet as a nation we've shot ourselves in the foot. We've made thinking outside the box so hip, so honored, and so rewarded—justly or not—that we have a stampede of young souls who want to be outside the box merely because they're told it makes them special.

The problem is that we're desperately hurting for people—young and old—who have mastered thinking *inside* the box.

I'm certainly not anti-creativity, nor anti-spontaneity. Remember that as an author, a speaker, and a 30-plus-year host in entertainment radio, creativity is my life blood. But we've endowed thinking outside the box with such a god-like status that we have generations of young people who feel as if they're a nobody if they're not focused on being exceptionally different in all ways, at all times. Why bother to spell correctly? Don't you realize my spelling is outside the box? Sorry, I'm not able to make correct change for your dollar, but I'm way too outside the box for that.

Call me a cultural speed bump, but I believe that we need to earn the right to step out of the box. Imagine if you will a society where nobody mastered anything considered inside the box. What if we all were contrarian? Do you see the inherent paradox there? A world where everyone is *outside the box* is chaos. Oh, what I wouldn't give for a solid mass of folks who were superb at all of those icky tasks that are necessary within the box. Most of our country's greatest creations came from minds that had perfected the skills inside the box before they emigrated to the outer limits. They could add and spell and articulate their thoughts. They didn't fall out of their crib with some expectation of outside-the-box entitlement. They earned their inner-box stripes, so to speak.

Of course, it's difficult to put the genie back in the bottle, and, quite frankly, there are so many people trumpeting their outside the box thinking that it has become a bit boring. Yes, we get it: you're very interesting. Just like everyone else.

In an age where a rebel becomes lost in a sea of rebels, where we push every child out of the box before they even understand the insides of it, I'd like to nominate the inside-the-box champions as our new heroes. We need them. And we need more students today to emulate them.

## Follow the leader

But wait, you say. How can young people be afflicted both by a desire to be unique, and by a desire to follow someone else? Because they're human, and they're no different than many adults. *Claiming* to be a rebel is often as good as being one.

During each of my school assemblies I like to watch the students as they file into the gym or the auditorium. They exhibit the ultimate pack mentality, always sauntering into the room in groups of four or five. And always with one person directing the action, deciding where they'll all sit, always in the center of the group, and usually the loudest.

Young adults swarm around the person who takes command, and they look to this person for guidance in many areas: fashion, tech trends, and pop culture interests. Remember Amanda from earlier in the chapter? I'm sure there was one person in particular in her peer group who was boisterous enough about those musical artists that Amanda was drawn into the whirlpool.

When it comes to attitudes, however, including the perception of education, this young leader holds a much more damaging influence over the students within the sphere. Follow the leader is fun when you're playing in the kindergarten schoolyard; it's potentially devastating for pliable middle school students.

There are thousands of books and articles devoted to the psychology of leadership. There are countless studies that attempt to explain why some people are natural born leaders, while most others are not only content with following, but who actually prefer it. For young adults the phenomenon is most often studied in relation to gang activity, where troubled, confused, and angry kids are swallowed up by a culture that makes no bones about its hierarchy, including a celebrated leader.

Even parenting experts will tell you that young adults might seem to push back against authority, but that deep down they're actually craving structure and guidance. They're looking for someone to follow.

This explains why all it takes is one gregarious student to corrupt a flock of young minds. Yes, as a parent you might have instilled a love of books and an interest in learning. But that was then; your child's *now* involves pack leaders who hold sway in what he thinks and how he behaves. Your child may be outgoing, and may have a mind of his own, but he's still subject to the forces of human nature. Through a strong desire to fit in, he's vulnerable to the influences of a leader who isn't likely to share many of your views and values.

And it's tough for kids to break away from the pack because they fear being ostracized. They'll unfortunately follow a leader down the wrong path because the other option means going it alone. And when you're fourteen, that's a scary proposition.

In some respects, though, the mindset of playing Follow The Leader can play to our benefit. As you'll see in Chapter 4, one of the challenges with education today involves finding brave leaders who will make academic excellence cool. For now, however, it helps us to recognize that a herd mentality contributes to the serious problem we have today.

# Failure to see the future

One of the biggest trends in the adult self-help category in the past few years has been the concept of living in the *now*. Millions upon millions of books, both traditional and audio, have been sold in an attempt to get people to live in the now. The authors tell us that we must stop obsessing over the past, and to quit worrying about a future that's out of our control anyway. Live in the moment, they say, enjoy what's going on now. It's all about NOW.

I think this is good advice for our stressed-out, over-scheduled, over-caffeinated adult world. We seem to spin out of control when we get caught up in the past and the future, and it often means that we lose focus on what's going on today. I'm guilty of it, and you probably are, too.

But with kids, the problem is that they can *only* focus on the now. Your average middle school student is so obsessed with what's going on around her at this very moment that she has no ability to contemplate what might happen tomorrow, and certainly not five years from now. Her universe is *today*, and she's completely absorbed in herself and what her friends find hot right now. This is the reason so many parents shake their heads and ask things like "What were you thinking? Didn't you think of the consequences?"

They weren't thinking about consequences because their brains aren't hard-wired to look more than five minutes down the road. They can't imagine how what they do today influences tomorrow. And that's a huge predicament when dealing with their education. In a teen's mind, how he behaves in the classroom and his attitude toward his studies has nothing to do with his future. He only knows that all of the adults around him seem to think it's important.

Of course, this leads to trouble later, and it obviously accounts for a great deal of a parent's frustration, because adults have learned to connect the dots; young adults haven't. And if you attempt to impress upon a teenager the fallout from their poor choices today, they'll often tune you out because they simply haven't had that program installed yet, and to them it sounds like white noise. You understand the concept of long-term consequences, but they don't. They understand *now*.

Of the four F's in this section, I believe this last one is the biggest culprit of them all in undermining education. It's why the other three have so much power. A teenager wouldn't fake it if they could see what would happen as a result; they wouldn't place so much emphasis on trying to be a rebel if they saw how worthless that strategy might be down the road; and they wouldn't follow a leader if they saw the cliff looming up ahead. Their inability to visualize the consequences of their actions enables them to make poor choices, especially those at school.

The good news is that there are solutions, and coming up I'll show you some of the ways I address them. Now that we've pulled back the veil on the Who, What, When, Where, and Why, we're ready to tackle the complex issue of personality.

# CHAPTER 4

# THE PERSONALITY FACTOR

No young adult chooses to be stupid, at least not intentionally. They're not looking at the big picture and then checking the box that handicaps them for life. Instead, they're opting for a lifestyle choice that neglects a valuable education in favor of more peer-approved outcomes based on image or popularity. To an average middle school or high school student, it's a matter of being swept along with the current, without much forethought to the consequences. The result, sadly, is often disastrous.

With that in mind, what aspects of a student's personality might influence how vulnerable they'll be to this peer pressure? As a parent or teacher, aren't you curious to understand what's ticking inside your children's heads, to discover what might be contributing to their attitudes and their behavior? While I'm not trained as a psychologist, I certainly recognize the importance of the field as it relates to the issue of student vulnerability to peer pressure. I offer this particular chapter to help adults understand how elements of personality come into play. If you're like me, three particular elements might very well resonate from your own personal experience, and lead to an a-ha moment:

- ✓ The Big Five Traits
- ✓ Introverts and Extraverts
- ✓ Fear of Failure

There have been countless studies and research papers that examine the role of personality in academic achievement, going back more than forty years. The bulk of the studies that I've found concentrate on university students, perhaps because the bulk of the papers are written by university students and professors, and willing participants are scattered around the campus. However, there have been a significant number that address the personality angle among elementary and secondary school students, as well.

We celebrate our differences, as we should. At the same time, those differences create challenges when we try to develop comprehensive education programs. It's very apparent that one size does not fit all. If you think it's tough for a classroom of twenty to thirty students, try managing schools of several thousand, and school districts with tens of thousands. Thousands of individuals with unique skills, abilities, learning styles, and personalities.

## The Big Five Traits

Personality differences have been the focus of extensive studies, often based on what contemporary psychologists refer to as The Big Five. These are the five traits that leading specialists use to define an individual's personality. Sometimes referred to as OCEAN—or, CANOE—they are:

**Openness**—Specifically, openness to experience, often expressed as an interest in art or music, as well as an inherent curiosity about new experiences.

**Conscientiousness**—Relating to responsibility and self-discipline; strength in this area might manifest as a tendency to plan rather than rely on spontaneous behavior.

**Extraversion**—Seen as energetic and positive, often seeking stimulation through interaction with others.

**Agreeableness**—Cooperation and compassion with others, rather than aggressive and/or antagonistic behavior.

**Neuroticism**—Sensitive and/or nervous, often quick to experience negative emotions, such as anger or depression.

The five traits are usually scored as a percentage, meaning that someone who scores only in the tenth percentile for extraversion is likely to enjoy quiet and solitude. Beneath each of these five there are various sub-categories that further tweak a person's makeup. So for every ten people examined, you'll have ten separate—and unique—makeups, each coloring the manner in which that person absorbs and processes information. And while you might think that genetics would play a dominant role in determining a person's scores, findings suggest that environment plays a surprisingly large role, too. For the sake of this book and the work I do with students, I was interested to learn how the multitude of possibilities affected classroom behavior and, ultimately, academic achievement.

According to several researchers, including a team from Southern Illinois University in 2008, conscientiousness plays perhaps the biggest role in determining a student's academic success. A high self-efficacy quotient of a student—how motivated they are to achieve success within a challenging environment—consistently is shown as an important factor in academic achievement.

Remember, conscientiousness is often described using terms such as thoroughness, organization, discipline, and—this is key— need for achievement. Almost without fail, whenever I address class- rooms of "gifted" students—a term that I personally feel is awkward and misnamed—I find that one of the characteristics they seem to share is an eagerness to achieve and succeed. Granted, it's anecdotal, but I doubt that it's coincidental. I firmly believe that some students, like some people in general, are wired to win, at any cost. When I think of students who are the least likely to succumb to negative academic peer pressure, it has to be the kids who are conscientious. In their minds, failure is abhorrent.

Researchers from The Groningen Institute for Educational Research in The Netherlands studied nearly 20,000 American students in Grade 7 and up. After controlling for outside factors such as ethnicity, gender, and even cognitive abilities, they found a definite correlation between Conscientiousness and Agreeableness and positive homework habits. Their report, published in 2010, found that students who scored high in self-discipline and cooperation spent more time on homework. Of course, one can argue that time spent on homework might not necessarily equate to a better learning experience; in fact, in some cases more homework time led to lower grades. But given the choice of spending quality time or little time on homework, which would you suspect produces better results?

And, as if to drive home the point, the same study showed a link between Conscientiousness and Agreeableness and higher end-of-term grades. In their summary, the authors stated that personality has a direct effect on grades.

To be fair, critics of the Big Five traits point out that it's too easy to oversimplify the characteristics. Also, one must take into account the variables of individuals reacting to specific circumstances.

Other personality factors come into play. In 2007 a team from Texas A&M University noted that resiliency also played an important role in student success, as early as first grade. In other words, a student's aptitude for bouncing back from a negative experience helps her to succeed where other students might become despondent and give up. I've spoken with school counselors about this ability to bounce back, and some have referenced its impact in fighting back against academic bullying.

But even taking bullying out of the equation, it's critical for young people to recognize the power of perseverance. Academic success comes easily to a special few, but for most students it's determined through effort and by practicing positive study skills. And with a national epidemic of dumbing down, it has become much too easy for a middle school or high school student to give up at the first sign of difficulty or at the first hint of peer ridicule.

As a side note: The same A&M researchers addressed another element in education that I believe is crucial for parents to understand. When it came to classroom readiness, teachers of very young students (kindergarten and first grade, primarily) indicated that the most valuable characteristics were enthusiasm and curiosity. In fact, they rated them even ahead of natural cognitive ability.

Enthusiasm and curiosity: exactly the two traits in short supply among middle school students who fall victim to academic peer pressure. Once a seventh-grader becomes convinced that it's uncool to be smart, his enthusiasm for school evaporates, and his innate curiosity is shelved. Because of this, it's critical that parents and teachers recognize the individual personality traits of their students; those who struggle with resiliency or self-motivation might be more vulnerable to outside influence—especially of the negative variety. They become easy targets for unmotivated students to drag down.

Another factor reported by psychologists is Academic Self-Concept (ASC), the personal beliefs that a student develops in regard to their own academic skills. This sometimes is mistakenly confused with self-esteem, but they're not the same. ASC embodies actual beliefs in an ability ("I'm a good writer"), while self-esteem is often centered around feelings. ASC has been referred to as self-efficacy, whereupon a student displays strong belief in their competency in a given situation.

Studies have indicated that Academic Self-Concept begins developing as early as age three. What's important to note is that many psychology experts believe that ASC can be influenced by environmental factors, meaning that it's possible for peer influences to impact a child's perception of her own abilities. She'll use others' opinions of her academic talents as a mirror, and—this is important—she'll believe them to be true. If this is accurate, it explains why so many straight A students in elementary school quickly shift as they immerse themselves in a middle school's social world, where peer influence not only supplies pressure in areas such as smoking, drinking, and sex, but in academics, as well. As parents and teachers, we hate to think that a child's Academic Self-Concept can be nudged the wrong way. That's powerful, and potentially dangerous.

## Introverts and Extraverts

There's a wealth of research regarding the classic personality models of introversion and extraversion, going back to Swiss psychiatrist Carl Jung. In the early twentieth century he popularized the idea of psychic energy flows and their correlation to a person's reserved or outgoing traits. While there are various definitions—and their accompanying lists of characteristics—most explanations generally adopt the notion that one is gregarious while the other less social. Psychologists, on the other hand, often state that most people lie somewhere in the middle, sharing components of both, although generally favoring one or the other.

The average person sees it as a fairly simple concept: extraverts (sometimes spelled extroverts) are outgoing people, and introverts are shy. In an opinion piece for *The New York Times,* however, author Susan Cain noted that introverts are not necessarily shy. In fact, she pointed out, there are four quadrants at work in this equation: calm introverts, anxious introverts, calm extraverts, and anxious extraverts. It's more a matter of where people derive their energy, their drive.

Jung's concept of energy flow began to make sense to me when it was explained like this: an extravert receives their power and energy from people and things around them, while an introvert is powered primarily from within. You're free to argue whether this is true or not, but for the sake of the discussion I hope we can agree on the basic premise.

With that in mind, I began to question the connection between these personality characteristics and academic achievement. Or, more specifically, whether an introvert or an extravert was more likely to be influenced academically by her peers. I found numerous studies and research papers on the subject of personality and academic success—with sometimes contradictory findings, naturally—but finding a paper that addresses the role of introvert/extravert qualities in dumbing down is another matter. Again, I offer my disclaimer that I'm untrained as a psychologist. I am, however, someone with twenty years of classroom involvement and observation, and someone who is passionately involved in a search for answers.

I'm most interested in the research findings that show little or no difference in IQ between outgoing and reserved individuals. That tells us that there's more than just basic intelligence at work here; there's another factor that either inhibits or supports one's motivation to succeed academically. I argue that it's the social element, one of the primary dividing lines between introverts and extraverts. Granted, the bulk of my argument is based upon anecdotal evidence, but I firmly believe that it passes the common-sense test.

Let's start with an examination of siblings. Take almost any family you know and ask the parents about their children. If there are two or more, I'm willing to bet that mom and dad say that no two of them are alike when it comes to personality. In a fascinating article for NPR, Alix Spiegel interviewed university professors and researchers, including a Darwin scholar, and the experts said it boiled down to three primary reasons.

One, competition within families leads children to focus on an area that the other children might have ignored. It's why an older sibling might be a terrific musician, while the younger child instead targets the athletic field. Competition has driven evolutionary change for millions of years; there's no reason why it wouldn't have an impact within family units. If my older brother is a football champion, I might look for an area where I won't walk in his shadow. Sometimes that leads to art, sometimes to academics. Or both.

Two, the timing involved in the children's lives is different. It might seem that three kids are all raised at about the same time, but it's usually not so. Conditions within the family change at different stages in the kids' lives; one might get through elementary school with an intact family, while another is just starting school when the parents separate. Or there's an illness that changes things. Or a move. Or any one of countless environmental subtleties that impact the personality of a child, and they're changes that can strongly influence a shift for one particular sibling.

And three, it's often a matter of perspective. While everyone in a given family might be gregarious, by comparison one might be slightly more outgoing. Thus, the other child—while perhaps traditionally viewed as an extravert—could be perceived as an introvert, purely from running in the shadow of a more socially-exuberant sib.

In any event, we're able to observe how these personality differences often correspond with a contrast in academic achievement. I'm friends with a family with two children, daughters who are separated in age by a mere sixteen months. The two girls look alike, they're both bright kids, and they're both athletic. Their personalities, however, could hardly be more dissimilar. The younger daughter is the epitome of a social butterfly, with a seemingly endless supply of friends. She's loud and assertive, even prone to break into song—loudly—at random times.

Her older sister, by comparison, is much more introspective. She tends to be the inquisitive one in the family, and can be relatively obsessive regarding organization. While her sister is singing, the older sibling is reorganizing her school folders.

When it comes to their academics, they also have little in common. The older, quieter sister carries a 4.0 GPA; the younger, socially-active sister struggles to maintain a B-average, and is regularly guilty of not turning in assignments. She spends an inordinate amount of time having to do makeup work.

Two young women with the same genes, the same home environment, and the same schools. And yet two drastically different academic paths. One very open to education and achievement, the other interested only in the social element of school. I know without hesitation which one would be the most likely to fall prey to another student's toxic attitude about education. You do, too, and I'm assuming that you also lack a PhD in psychology.

True, this is only one family, and it's hard to convince some people when the sample size is one. I get it. But I hear the same story repeated over and over again, where the extraverted child scores well in the social circles while the introvert wins in the classroom. Introverts, by their nature, carry a higher degree of conscientiousness. If you look up the definition of that specific personality trait, you'll see a line that reads: " . . . related to successful academic performance in students." Those are not my words; they're written by professionals.

Given our country's obsession with social media, it's fair to say that we celebrate an extraverted lifestyle. We even keep a detailed count of digital friends! When has that ever happened in history? It's time for us to consider that when a young person—especially one who is hard-wired as an extravert—carries a fascination with attention and social interaction, they're perhaps more likely to be distracted, to be knocked off their educational path. For a quiet and curious introvert, the drive for popularity is nowhere near as strong. They live much more inside their own heads. Gregory Feist, a professor at San Jose State University, says that introverts are "comfortable working in solitary conditions."

Some have suggested that introverts simply sift through information more thoroughly, patiently taking the time to absorb the data. They're often uncomfortable working through a problem in a group setting, preferring to use their own cognitive abilities to solve an issue. Steve Wozniak, one of the founders of the Apple corporation, compared engineers and inventors—obviously two sets of very bright people—to artists, in that they create their best work when working alone; "not on a committee," he said. "Not on a team."

In other words, they don't feed off the power of the group. Instead, like other introverts, they dig down for the inspiration and motivation to achieve. I believe it's the same way for middle school students: some keep their heads down and drive forward, while others are more socially conscious, more apt to seek friendship and acceptance by their peers. I look back at my own days in middle school, and recall these exact same feelings. When I was left to tackle a project on my own, I was happiest; when given a group assignment, such as you might find with lab partners in science class, I was much more ill at ease.

I'm not arguing that one is more intelligent than the other; on the contrary, study after study supports the notion that extraverts have just as much—and sometimes more—intellectual drive as introverts. It's a question of who might be more susceptible to academic peer pressure. And it might very well explain why parents nod in agreement when discussing their quite-different children, where one is a quiet academic high-achiever, while the other, more socially-gifted child struggles in the classroom. It's possible that children who are extraverts run more of a risk of succumbing to the inexorable tug of the cool crowd, the popular crowd, the crowd that feels that "only dorks read."

## Fear of failure

In November of 2011 I spoke at a gathering of educators in Chicago. It was the Assembly on Literature for Adolescents (ALAN) conference, which traditionally is scheduled during the annual gathering of the National Council of Teachers of English (NCTE). As a speaker, you're before hundreds of teachers and librarians, many of whom want to hear about the hottest new young adult/teen books for their schools. The group is also, as you might imagine, very tuned in to anything that touches on literacy issues in general. It was a perfect venue for me to stand at the podium and discuss the mission of The Big Brain Club. I delighted in sharing a message that Smart Is Cool, and was buoyed by the multiple interruptions of applause.

I especially enjoyed the fascinating one-on-one discussions that took place before and after my presentation. Teachers are accustomed to being the targets of politicians and parents who are desperate to find someone to blame for our nation's academic woes, so these educators were very happy to open up and share their personal observations of classroom behavior to someone who is genuinely interested in finding workable solutions.

One teacher in particular, whom I guessed to be in her mid- to late-thirties, cornered me afterward seeking additional information about my non-profit education foundation, The Big Brain Club. My nature, in that situation, is to probe for information, to find out what exactly today's educators are encountering in their classrooms. She and I began talking about the personality differences between high-achieving students and those who had adopted more of an "I don't care" attitude.

"Many times it's fear of failure," she told me. I found her explanation—which I'll paraphrase here—very interesting.

Essentially, she said, too many people confuse a child's fear of failure with a lack of self-esteem, and although that plays a small role—as we'll soon see—they're not the same thing. These kids, in her opinion, feel good about themselves, and they're generally confident in many areas. These are not young people who wallow in insecurity; indeed, they're often very open—and effusive—in their self-praise.

No, this is an element of their personality that never wants to experience failure in any way. The result is that they consciously choose to coast through school, to the point of even neglecting their education. If that sounds contradictory—which is what I originally suggested— this teacher's observation is that some young adults are fearful of always having to "live up to expectations." In other words, it's better to coast through school with B's and C's, which requires little effort, than to try to consistently produce strong grades. There's a part of their personality which is so afraid of failure that they'll elect to ignore their studies in order to fit in with the bulk of the crowd.

A phrase jumped into my mind, and I shared it with this teacher: "The anonymity of mediocrity." She nodded with a wry smile. She's watched it play out many times, often with students who she knows are intelligent and talented; they elect to dumb down in order to fit in with the crowd, thereby never setting themselves up for failure.

In psychological terms it's known as Self-Handicapping, and defined as avoiding effort in an attempt to save one's self-esteem. This behavior has been the subject of many books, primarily aimed at workers, business executives in particular. Career coaches are familiar with people trying to climb the corporate ladder, but who short-circuit those efforts by avoiding anything that involves sticking their neck out. It's also sometimes connected with a condition known as Avoidance Behavior.

Those who earn a living by coaching others through troubled romantic relationships—or through periods where finding a dating partner has been difficult—witness similar behavior. They're coaching people who won't give completely of themselves for fear that the relationship will eventually fail anyway, and they don't want to get hurt.

So while it's common in adults, within their careers and their relationships, it makes complete sense that we would find similar behavior in young people. The difference for students, however, is that rather than showing up as a career crisis, it reveals itself in their world of school work and social networks. Impressionable middle school students are already going through one of the more difficult transitional periods of their lives, where they're changing physically and emotionally; now throw in a new complication, whereby they attribute dumbing down to simply "playing it safe."

Former Secretary of Health, Education, and Welfare John W. Gardner once said, "One of the reasons people stop learning is that they become less and less willing to risk failure."

It's a challenge for parents and teachers to recognize this element of a young adult's personality, and to nudge them toward a new way of thinking. Professionals who work with adults in mitigating Self-Handicapping understand that the key is often developing trust. For students who show signs of succumbing to academic peer pressure, it's important to work on two levels of trust.

The first involves building trust in their education in general, which means helping young people to understand the real reason they're going to school. You might think that sounds funny, but it's true: more kids than you can imagine have never really connected the dots between their education and their outcome. I've often asked young people, "Why do you go to school?" After the funny looks, few of them respond with anything close to the real answer: To prepare them for their future. It becomes a matter of building trust in what they're working toward. Sometimes that's a quicker conversation than you might think, although it requires constant reinforcement.

And then there's the matter of building individual trust in their own abilities. Athletic coaches are very familiar with the concept, and consistently apply it on the practice field. But how many young people ever hear the message as it pertains to their education?

Education conferences often feature sessions on connecting with students, especially the "hard-to-reach" student. I'm glad to see that some schools go beyond this step, and also invest time and training in helping teachers to build an individual student's trust in their own talents. It's a strategy that parents would be wise to follow at home, too, because it presents an extremely valuable learning moment.

I'm a goal setter. I write down my goals in everything from spiral notebooks to digital notebooks to whiteboards. I'll admit that I rarely reach the 100% completion mark; either the pages get crossed out in the notebook, or the digital file is deleted, or the whiteboard is erased. But I immediately follow-up with a new set of goals, and I think my overall achievement rate is fairly high.

The key, in my opinion, is that I'm not afraid to set the goal high. Michelangelo warned us that the greatest danger wasn't that we aimed high and missed, but that we aimed low and reached it. I'm convinced that one of the greatest gifts a parent or teacher can pass along to a young person is a heart-to-heart (or several of them) regarding their aim, instilling a commitment to excellence. True, they might occasionally miss the mark, but I'd rather bet on an ambitious goal setter than someone who is content to just sneak by.

If students are apt to blow off their education because they're afraid to fail, we've got important work to do. There are countless examples, all very inspiring, of great people who took great falls before achieving great things. We all know in our guts that these people are the ones who aimed high, who weren't afraid of ridicule. It breaks my heart to imagine a supremely talented middle school student who throws away a bright future because of his fear of failure.

Not to get too quote-heavy, but I also appreciate Sir Ken Robinson's outlook. The author and speaker practically echoed the mantra of my education foundation, The Big Brain Club, when he said: "Helping people to connect with their personal creative capacities is the surest way to release the best they have to offer."

And that's what it's all about: not simply helping young people to get good grades, but to help them to become the best version of themselves. That's something they can't do if they sell themselves short. Or, even worse, if they allow someone else to stifle their potential.

# MARCUS

**"I was the obnoxious loudmouth."**

Sitting across the booth from this mild-mannered, well-groomed, and exceedingly courteous man, it was difficult to imagine the younger version of himself that he laid out for me. And yet, his story was on track with those that millions of adults could tell, providing the unique perspective that time allows.

Marcus is now in his forties, a loving father of two daughters, and a businessman. He's trim and well-dressed, with eyes that take in everything around him with a quiet coolness, analyzing his surroundings, while still politely engaged in our discussion. His dialogue is punctuated with *please, thank you,* and even an occasional *yes sir.* I can tell that he's genuinely interested in the thread of our talk, allowing him to not only contribute his personal experiences, but perhaps at the same time providing him with a bit of insight into his turbulent past.

The path which led Marcus from rebellious teen to responsible adult included a stint in juvenile court. He dropped out of school not once, but twice. Given the circumstances of his chaotic adolescence, I got the feeling that even he is somewhat surprised at how his life eventually unfolded.

During the course of our conversation, he used the words "peer pressure" more than a few times. Sometimes it related to those obnoxious, loudmouth days, but I noticed how it characterized a *positive* turn in his life, too. It's funny, but we tend to automatically associate the words with negative, destructive behavior—especially when observing young people—but for Marcus they represent both his choppy descent and his triumphant revival, a tale that places him, ironically, on both sides of the law.

One of seven kids growing up, he described a family history that's all too familiar for millions of Americans: a troubled home life, a father with a drinking problem, an uneducated mother. There was a palpable disdain for education inside the home; only one sibling attended college, and Marcus couldn't help but hear the sneering comments from his father, denigrating the one child who sought this better life, making it clear that being a "college boy" was garbage. There was no academic encouragement, let alone help, to be found. Kindergarten was considered "unnecessary," which meant that Marcus was already behind by the time he walked into his first grade class. Not surprisingly, he was held back to repeat that first year.

By the time he reached junior high school, Marcus discovered a way to make mandatory school time more entertaining. He became a class clown, a rebellious student whose principal goal was to make friends, and to make them laugh. Pranks became his trademark, often targeting the teachers at his school. He shook his head when recalling the theft of a horse, which—a la Animal House—was led into the school and locked inside the janitor's office.

But there was more: alcohol, marijuana, theft of neighbors' property. And, of course, ditching school. He was thirteen and on the downward slope.

To this day, he acknowledges that landing in juvenile court was the wake-up call. He was assigned to a counselor who monitored his movements and evaluated his progress in school. And yet even that might have failed to correct his course if it hadn't been for one particular teacher who stepped up and made a suggestion that changed the young man's life.

Woody, as the junior high school teacher was known to his students, put his arm around Marcus and told him about an organization called the Alpine Rescue Team. Essentially a search and rescue outfit in the Rocky Mountains, they often picked up the slack where fire departments were unable to respond. They handled high-altitude rescues, avalanche patrolling, and other coordinated mountain details. Woody was a volunteer with the group, and strongly encouraged Marcus and some of his friends to give it a shot. Needless to say, they were reluctant.

But an alarm was going off inside the adolescent boy's mind. With no supervision or discipline at home, dismal results at school, and with a court appearance already on his record, he knew that he could either continue to sabotage his future, or he could push away from the pressure to be "the popular kid" and focus on what really mattered: real life.

You're probably already a step ahead, and have realized that Marcus enrolled in the Alpine Rescue program. You're right. You've probably also concluded that it was somehow good for him. You're right again. But it's the reason *why* it worked that's not only interesting, but further evidence of the power behind peer pressure, both negative and positive.

Marcus was thrust into a world of adult responsibility, and, more importantly, *critical* responsibility. This was no longer a game, and there were no fellow teenage boys standing around snickering; lives were literally on the line. There were no do-overs.

And he was surrounded by responsible adults, each of whom demanded results. As he told me: "I had to grow up quickly. I had to be mature."

Now, instead of sleep-walking through school and basking in the warmth of being the popular slacker, he'd found something special. "It became the center of my universe," he said. And, a metamorphosis began. "I was an important person, but for a better reason."

*An important person for a better reason.*

Marcus finally looked up from the miasma of his juvenile surroundings. Something clicked, something which—for the first time in his life—allowed him to look beyond the short-term waste he'd made of his education.

**But it wasn't a complete evolution.** Not yet.

Marcus began high school, and promptly discovered that he was still unhappy. His new-found experience in the real-world had whetted his appetite, and he longed to experience more of it. The structure that he'd discovered with the search and rescue team didn't apply in his classrooms, and soon his interest in school waned again. Following a disagreement with a math teacher, he hit bottom, and dropped out of school.

For the next month he took a job as a roofer, and once again found structure and discipline. But, as he said, "common sense told me that I had to go back to school. I didn't want to be a roofer for the rest of my life." So, giving up the well-paying job, he loaded up his backpack and trudged back to school. But his return lasted until lunch; he dropped out a second time on his first day back.

Now he'd reached a crossroads in his life. An internal battle raged between his naturally rebellious, sarcastic side and his rational mind, the side struggling to mature in a complicated setting that included both peers and working adults.

His next step was to investigate an alternative high school. Limited to only 100 students, the principal was helpful in showing him around and touting the school's benefits, but he was also blunt about the chances of getting in. There was a lengthy waiting list. Marcus began to wonder how he'd ever finish school.

Without officially enrolling, he hung around day after day, sitting in on classes as a guest. During lunch breaks he chatted with teachers and some of the students, and immediately felt a connection. He was intrigued by the school's approach to education. Students were given assignments, and were allowed to work within their own structure. But it was not a free pass to goof off; you were given five years to get your work finished in order to graduate. If not, you were gone, and there would be no second chance.

"The atmosphere made me want to learn, to want to be there," he said. "And there was no peer pressure."

Marcus touched on another important point. "The students' attitude about education was different because they *chose* to be there. They were there for different reasons, but they had responsibilities. You had to get the work done, however it worked for you."

After finding out about his experience with search and rescue, an instructor at the school asked Marcus if he'd help teach a class on the subject. Of course, if they were going to ask him to teach, the least they could do was allow him to enroll.

Marcus graduated in two years, not five. From there, he began a career in emergency services, training as an EMT and a firefighter, before signing on with a police force. And, in an ironic unfolding of destiny, the troubled young man who had scoffed at education—dropping out twice—traveled from juvenile court to his eventual job as the chief of police of a small mountain town. The climb that Marcus embarked upon was both literal and figurative; his journey up the mountain mirrored his ascent from despair to success.

**Today he marvels at what might have been** had he not escaped from the suffocating pressure that he felt from his peers. He'd lived to entertain his friends, even at the expense of his education and his future, coming dangerously close to a dead-end that would have assured him a difficult go at life.

But it was a different form of pressure that brought him around. Instead of pressure to dumb down, Marcus was introduced to *expectations*. No longer was it important to make his peers snicker; suddenly he was in a world where he was expected to perform, both in his work with the Alpine Rescue Team, and with the alternative school program that he joined.

We don't always associate the word *expectations* with pressure, but it's simply an internal pressure that we apply ourselves. We base it on the conclusions that we draw from our environment, whether it's education or work. Our own expectations drive us toward a much healthier plan of action than those derived from others' expectations for us. Marcus perhaps needed a jolt from the juvenile court system to see the light, but it was a teacher who recognized what a difference a mature environment could make for a troubled young man.

# CHAPTER 5

# THE DARK SIDE
# OF TECHNOLOGY

I was visiting with a friend's daughter, and one of the daughter's friends, each sophomores in high school. During our discussion the Declaration of Independence somehow came up, and, just out of curiosity, I asked the daughter what year the Declaration had been signed.

She had no idea.

For a few minutes, she and the friend threw out various guesses, ranging from 1850 to 1910. Eventually it got to the point where they were simply offering dates, with no basis for their guesses. When I finally asked them if the year 1776 rang a bell at all—did it register for any particular reason in their heads?—they both said no.

Before we go much further, keep this in mind: both of these girls are honor students at their high school.

Of course, I expressed surprise that they had maneuvered through ten years of schooling—successfully, according to the standards—without recognizing what is arguably the most important date in our nation's history. Their response cuts straight to the heart of this chapter: "We can always look it up."

Kind of eye-opening, isn't it? We can't deny that the gadgets and other technology advances of the last few years influence us. That "us," by the way, includes both adults and students, but, in the case of young people and their education, the influence works as an element in our nation's problem with dumbing down. In this chapter I'll address some of the factors that swing back and forth between helpful and hurtful, and how they impact a young person's path.

✓ The Replacements

✓ Knowing Versus Knowing Where

✓ The Value Question

**I should state up front** that I'm not a hand-wringer when it comes to technology. I don't cry that "things were better in a simpler time," because I don't believe that they were. You'll never hear me utter the phrase "good old days," because I'm convinced that nostalgia is a one-sided proposition, elevating the quaint goodness of the times while downplaying—or flat-out ignoring—the hardship and inconvenience. We tend to only remember the good, thus romanticizing some vague past.

But when it comes to education, I understand how the frustration that many of us feel over the outcomes can be directed at—and attributed to—our digital devices. I just don't buy into that. The devices themselves could be the greatest things that ever happened to education, if . . .

The big If. As with any invention, it's how you use it. Are you prepared to accept a world where technology changes even how we *define* education? You'd better be.

## The Replacements

On our radio show I once admitted to feeling sadness when I traded in one thing for another. Some people get a new car every two or three years, but I'm the kind of guy who drives the same vehicle for six to ten years. And no matter how shiny and nice the new car is, when

I see the dealer drive my old one away, I watch until it disappears from sight, with a definite pain in my heart.

Judging from the phone calls to our show, I'm not alone. One woman told me that she wept when she bought a new washer and dryer.

The look of education is changing, with many traditional tools and practices being replaced by the shiny new device and sparkly new methods. We can either cry about them, and lament the loss of the old ways, or recognize the value and benefit of what's new.

This is not your old Maytag anymore.

One example involves books, something school kids have been lugging around for centuries. Today's traditional books are being replaced by digital copies, volumes that can be accessed on e-readers or a student's phone. And with the trajectory of change escalating at a steeper and steeper angle (see Ray Kurzweil's writing in *The Singularity Is Near*), children born in 2013 and later may rarely come into contact with an old-style book, perhaps looking at them as later generations view cassettes or eight-track tapes.

But it's not just that the format of the books has changed. The feel of reading has morphed, in a way making it seem like a different experience.

My elementary school years explain much of what would later become an integral part of my life. The son of a military man, I was used to moving every couple of years; uprooted from one school and one group of friends, and moved around the country—or around the world—to a new setting. Other than my family, there was one constant that stood out: books. I buried myself in mysteries and science fiction, and to this day I credit Isaac Asimov, Arthur C. Clarke, and the Hardy Boys for keeping me company in a strange land. One of my biggest thrills was walking into the library, knowing that an immense world of adventure was waiting. I'd walk out with the maximum number of books allowed, cradling them as the holy objects they were.

We had three television channels, no video games, no computers, no cell phones . . . but absolutely no worries. Stacks of books were treats. I swear, libraries even had a smell to them, a scent of books that I could still identify today with my eyes closed.

Yes, today there are still libraries, and I still love them. But there's a difference now for today's youth, and it's not because of the new technology itself; rather, it's how that technology has caused a mental shift. When you're allowed to go to the library once a week—particularly when it's just about all the escape available to you—it takes on a different aura than when it's available all the time.

Or when it's available at the push of a button.

Libraries to me as a kid were practically places of worship. When you're able to access your heaven on a device in your pocket, it loses much of its reverence. It's now always there; it's easy; and it has no feel or smell. Today's students have access to more information than we could've ever imagined. True, a large percentage of that "information" might be garbage—oh, the pros and cons of the Internet!—but there's something to be said for having complete dictionaries and encyclopedias at your fingertips, whether you're in the classroom, your kitchen, or · while you're hiking a mountain.

Our digital devices are replacements for learning the information in the first place.

For an extreme example, consider two people lost in the middle of nowhere, hikers who are stranded miles from civilization, awaiting a night of temperatures well below freezing. Our two trekkers come from different backgrounds: one has studied survival skills, and has learned how to build a fire and identify dangerous plants and animals; the other has a cell phone and knows where to go online to read all about starting a fire.

Except there's no Internet access now. Or, more likely, the battery on the phone is dead. With no shelter and no chance of rescue, who are you putting your money on to survive the night?

Again, it's an extreme example, but you can extrapolate the gist of the lesson here. Both hikers have information: one has actually learned the steps necessary to get by, and the other has learned where to digitally access the information that has been logged by others. Or, to put it more succinctly, one's information has considerably more value than the other's. The problem is, if you're twelve years old and you've never spent more than five minutes disconnected from the grid, you not only can't imagine a world without it, you see no difference in value between knowing something and knowing where to find it. And I challenge you to try to explain that difference without incurring a severe rolling of the eyes.

This is how technology contributes to the acceptance of dumbing down. I can't necessarily fault a teenager who laps up every new gadget and every new shortcut. Had these devices been available in my youth, I would've been just as absorbed. Nonetheless, it presents a challenge in tweaking the attitude of a young adult regarding knowledge and— more importantly—the attitude toward the *process* of acquiring that knowledge. Dumbing down is not only the cool way to go, it fails to strike fear into a student's heart because, to their way of thinking, there's always a safety net.

It might be one reason why the value of knowledge has declined. When you lose something, you feel the loss. When you never knew it to begin with, it has no power.

## Knowing Versus Knowing Where

I've hosted a particular feature on the radio for twenty years, one that has brought families together during their morning commutes to school, and one that gives co-workers something to talk about throughout the day. It's called *The Mindbender,* and it's easily the most popular radio feature with which I've ever been involved. In some ways it's become iconic, because there are parents of college-aged kids who can recall listening to *The Mindbender* when they drove that child to first grade. An entire generation essentially grew up with it.

Contrary to what outsiders might think, it's not trivia. With trivia, you either know it or you don't. "Who was the second president of the United States?" would be considered trivia, because you either know it was John Adams or you don't. With my radio feature, the questions are lifestyle-based, and you have a chance to either puzzle them out or simply guess; either way it's fun, and the answers that are called in often provoke a lot of laughter.

For example: "The average woman has nine pairs of shoes in her closet that all have this in common."

See, you probably don't know right off the top of your head, but you can at least play along. You know the answer isn't John Adams. (And, if the question is now lodged in your brain and you *must* know the answer, I'll share it with you in a few pages.)

But a funny thing happened to *The Mindbender* a few years ago. We host a live audience in our studio every Friday morning, another tradition that has been around for years. Ten people sit in on the show, and get to watch how it works from behind the scenes. We interact with them, and during commercial breaks we chat with them about the business and answer their questions about radio in general and our show in particular.

The audience enjoys watching *The Mindbender* performed live. Imagine my surprise several years ago when I tossed out the question one Friday morning, and watched a couple of the audience members immediately pull out their cell phones. At first I thought they were trying to call in—which, I have to admit, would be hilarious if they were able to actually get through and talk to us on the air from about ten feet away.

But no. Both of these people, adult women in their early twenties, were accessing the Internet and launching a search to try to find the answer. This was early in the era of phones with online capability, the first time people were able to carry a worldwide treasure of information in their purse or pocket. After a few minutes of searching—unsuccessfully, I might add—I asked them what they thought the answer was. They looked at each other, and then responded with a blank stare. They had no answer whatsoever.

You have to understand that *The Mindbender* is not hard science, there are no mathematical equations involved, and you don't need a college degree to play. You saw the question about the shoes; that's pretty much a typical question. But the two young women were stumped, unable to even *guess*, because they couldn't access any information online. Somehow, it seems, they'd lost their ability to process a question and formulate a response based on their own intuition and cognitive skills. Their knowledge base was now entirely dependent upon a digital database; in some respects, their reasoning abilities had atrophied.

This is the dark underside of our new reliance upon technology. Millions of students are coming of age in a world where it's not necessarily considered important to *know* something, as long as you know where to look it up. In fact, it has fueled a growing attitude that it's a waste of time to learn things; a growing knot of students will scoff at someone who bothers to learn those silly "facts" when it's completely unnecessary to do so. It adds a false sense of efficiency, confusing access to information with knowledge, and providing "cool" kids with yet another reason to ridicule a fellow student who goes the extra step.

What's lost in this digital evolution is the ability of students to think for themselves. Puzzling out facts and ideas might seem old school and dusty, but it also teaches the brain how to connect the dots. School is not just about learning the facts; it's about learning *how* to think. It's a system for stretching and exercising the mental muscles necessary to sort out the hows and whys of information gathering.

Scientists call it plasticity. In a nutshell, your brain is made up of tens of billions of neurons, and from the moment you're born these neurons begin building connections with each other. Learning involves linking, in other words, and the more those links are developed, the more things the brain is able to associate. Learn a new word, and a connection is made. Repeat the word several times, and use it in a sentence, and that connection is strengthened.

But our brains also subscribe to the "use it or lose it" template. As we move into our adolescent and teenage years, we strengthen some of our circuits while others begin to lapse. The plasticity of a healthy adult human brain is truly one of the most incredible wonders in our known universe, and, to quote a classic marketing campaign, it's a terrible thing to waste.

By sweeping a basic education into the waste basket and replacing it with a simple mantra of "just look it up online," we're destroying not just the basic foundation of a young mind, but also eliminating that mind's essential plasticity at an important early age. Without it, you end up with the blank looks I received in our live audience show. I honestly don't care if the young ladies knew the answer to The Mindbender or not; what troubled me was their inability to even contemplate an answer on their own. Important neural pathways didn't exist.

This is one part of the bigger picture of dumbing down, and why it has become acceptable for some young people. A crucial component of fitting in with the hip crowd involves technology. Not only do you need to possess the gadgets themselves, but you must be completely connected, up-to-date on the skills and shortcuts that define you as either cool or not. And today, the ability to search and find online is one of those shortcuts. It's helpful, no doubt, but in some respects it's robbing a young mind of its plasticity. What you're left with is a generation that will sacrifice its ability to think and process in order to be cool. And worse, they have no recognition of what they're even sacrificing. To them, knowing where to find information is the *only* way to do it. As the old saying goes, they don't even know what they don't know.

And to ask that they give up the convenience of looking up an answer has two problems. For one, it suggests to them that they do something the hard way instead of the easy way, which goes against our human nature. And secondly, it smacks of giving up their cool edge, which is an unheard of proposition. These are two more reasons why students who do work to actually learn the information are sometimes perceived as social outcasts and nerds. That pressure is enough to convince some impressionable young people to blow off their education, because it's just "not necessary."

I personally love the convenience of the web, and I'll use it to find data on a regular basis. But I also still have the ability to think my way through a problem in the absence of that digital connection, and again there's an element of pride involved. I'm proud of the fact that I can often work it out on my own, and it's this pride that has been lost for many teenagers.

And, by the way, what do those nine pairs of shoes have in common? The woman never wears them.

## The Value Question

Although her name has been changed, here's a true story about Kristen, an eighth grader in a public school. She's a very social creature, quick to make friends, and immersed in the new digital age of networking and posting. For her, school is mostly a place to see friends, but her grades place her roughly in the middle of the pack, neither spectacular nor failing.

One of her class projects centered around the periodic table, that classic layout of the known chemical elements, arranged by their atomic number. Each student was assigned a specific element, and charged with creating a variety of media in which to showcase it. Kristen drew boron, represented on the table by a capital B, with an atomic number of 5, nestled comfortably between beryllium and carbon.

Kristen diligently went to work crafting a Powerpoint presentation, complete with colorful slides and dissolving graphics. She also put together a simple folding brochure, highlighting the technical details of boron, and for good measure created a boron-influenced crossword puzzle. All in all, several hours worth of work went into her assignment, resulting in a collection of materials that were both creative and colorful. For her efforts she received an A from the teacher.

But let's go back to the day she turned it in. While driving to school, her mother noticed some of the materials and asked what it was all about. When Kristen told her that it was a class project on the table of elements, and that her assignment was boron, the mother casually asked Kristen about the metalloid.

Kristen's response: "I don't know."

Pressing, the mom asked for at least some minor details. For instance, where do we find boron? What's it used for?

Kristen's response: "I don't know."

And she wasn't simply being an obstinate teenager; she honestly couldn't tell her mother a single thing about her assignment. She did, however, learn how to sit at the computer and cut and paste pretty pictures into a Powerpoint presentation, and she was quite proud of the colorful brochure.

She knew absolutely nothing about the object of the exercise. Not a year later, not a month later; she knew nothing about boron the morning after she'd finished a week-long project. What's more, she looked at her mother as if she were crazy, as if to say, *Why do I need to know about boron?*

The heart of this issue lies within the concept of value. If a student understands that technology can make her life—including her education—easier, she'll be quick to adopt whatever fad and gadget will accomplish that. If a computer can facilitate cutting information from one source and pasting it onto another document—without wasting precious time by actually reading and absorbing the information—then she'll happily click her way to an A. This isn't a matter of whether we should use technology in our classrooms—I most definitely believe we should—it's a question of what value a student derives from the implementation of that technology. Not the value that they perceive, but rather the actual, objective value.

One can argue that value will always be purely subjective rather than objective, but in this case I think we can agree that Kristen acquired zero value on the study of boron. Remember, this wasn't a class assignment on creating slide shows or drawing brochures; it was a project allegedly geared toward learning about the table of elements and its constituent parts. Kristen received an A, and knew zero about her subject. That places the value of her knowledge on the subject at zero.

Recall the look that Kristen presented to her mother during the drive to school. The glossy sheen of her homework results meant the world to her, and likely would compare favorably to those in her peer group. The substance of her work, however, didn't register at all. She saw no value in the knowledge, and therefore felt no remorse whatsoever for failing to answer a single question about the element. To this eighth grader, value doesn't lie in the acquisition of knowledge, but rather in the polished look of the brochure, a two-fold pamphlet that—if she ever really needed to know about boron—could supply any information.

I'm aware that some people will take this section of *Smart Is Cool* and use it to argue the relative merits of some teachers, or use it to attack the curricula and/or lessons within public schools. To me that's an entirely different discussion, valid or not, and it misses the point. What's critical to the mission of The Big Brain Club and other like-minded organizations is the mindset of a middle school student and how they perceive the value of their education.

We tend to immediately assign a dollar figure when addressing issues of value, but look beyond the currency value and focus on the importance and usefulness. A car might very well have a resale value of $30,000, but when it's snowing at 5AM and I have to get across town to work, the value to me is a warm, reliable form of transportation. The sub sandwich might have a comparative value of five dollars, but when I'm hungry and the pantry is bare, it's a quick and tasty way to satisfy my need for fuel.

The value of education is often expressed in dollars, whether it's the cost per student in your town's public school system, or the price tag of an Ivy League four-year degree. It's also expressed as the sum of lifetime earnings based on one's level of education, i.e. the value of a high school diploma versus a college degree. But what about the intrinsic value of an education?

There are schools today that allow students to use either their textbooks or the Internet for each and every test. They're not asked to learn the information, but rather encouraged to become astute at looking things up. One fifteen-year-old told me that her class spent an entire week learning only how to use Google. For her, the value of her education exists only when she has access to the Internet. In an unplugged world, she would be lost. And yet, based on her experiences and those of her peers, it's not cool to spend hours learning the data buried within the bytes; she'll voluntarily dumb down to blend in with her digital compatriots, and never know—or care—what she's missing. The value of her education is . . . what?

**For years we've struggled with the rise of the machine,** and science fiction novels have frightened us with visions of future societies that are physically plugged into a global neural network. I am not suggesting that we cower in fear of computers and other devices, nor that we eliminate them from the classroom. On the contrary, my education foundation goes so far as to supply high-tech products to schools in order to help reach students who some have deemed "unreachable." I see the major benefits that technology can bestow upon our education system.

What I'm lobbying for is a shift in the way in which the devices are used. Rather than supplanting our need to learn, we would be wise to develop lesson plans that use digital servants to enhance the learning process. Although we're rapidly approaching the point where machines will surpass the human brain's processing power, at least for now we still possess the greatest computer in our known universe. It's a biological computer that thrives on exercise and plasticity, one that evolves when pushed to its limits and atrophies when neglected.

Students, by their nature, will often want the quick and easy path to an outcome, and technology certainly provides that path. It's in our best interests to govern the use of these tools in order for a student's natural tools to properly develop, and in order for them to understand and appreciate the value of knowledge.

CHAPTER 6

# THE CHALLENGE

W e've seen how this war began, and we've heard from the people on the front lines. Now it's time to see exactly what battles we need to fight in order to claim victory. Like any great conflict, it won't be easy. But as long as we know what we're up against—call it our intellectual reconnaissance—it can help us develop the necessary strategies.

These are the three primary challenges for The Big Brain Club, a list that cries out to be called The Three D's.

✓ Dismantling the negative stereotype of smart kids
✓ Discovering brave leaders
✓ Defining 'The Reward of the Challenge'

Of course, as with most difficult tasks, there are too many smaller challenges to list in one chapter, so we'll focus on these big three. They represent the brunt of the work cut out for us. Let's get going.

## Dismantling the negative stereotype of smart kids

Few people want to play on your team if you have a reputation for being perpetual losers. Few people want to work for your company if everyone in the industry bad-mouths you. Few people want to eat at your restaurant if all of the reviews are in the toilet.

So, if too many jokers out there—including many in the pop culture scene—have convinced impressionable kids that being smart is a sure way to be labeled a dork or a nerd, then we shouldn't be surprised when so many students check out of their education. It's too easy for them to sit back and coast their way through school.

Today, young people are quick to choose cool over intellect. Not long ago I passed a boy in his late teens, maybe early 20s, wearing a shirt with this statement splashed across the front: "Genius by birth, slacker by choice."

By choice. Young adults don't even hide the fact that they will gladly choose an underachieving life because it provides a certain amount of perceived prestige, the key word being *perceived*. And yet, ask them years later, and you get a much, much different story. In a poll of adults, conducted by Classmates.com, when asked to name their biggest regret from high school, more than sixty percent said that they wished they'd (a) studied harder, and (b) considered their future. Those were the top two answers.

It's easy to be a rebel when you're young. When you grow up a bit, the real world tends to intrude on those plans.

So the first challenge is to convince Mr. Slacker-By-Choice that he's making a wrong choice now. It doesn't do us much good if he finally figures it out at age 30 or (gulp) 40. And in order to get him to buy in, the stereotype of the Loser Nerd needs to be squashed.

It can't happen overnight, and it will never work with every young person. Let's be honest, no program will ever gain one hundred percent success. The key for The Big Brain Club is dismantling the negative image to the point where a sizable chunk of students have the hipster blinders removed. By doing so, we also remove the stigma that keeps them from pursuing a better life. Remember the story of Dylan from the Introduction? If he hadn't been told by all of his peers that Smart equals Uncool, he would've been fine.

If the older generation is serious about wanting a better life for their kids, one way they could help would be to stop glamorizing poor choices. Even when we get older, it seems, we discuss our past mistakes with a bit of a swagger. It somehow paints us as battle-scarred survivors, or well-seasoned miscreants. And again, let's be honest, it makes us look cool even to say we *used* to do those things. That's why we say it, not to impart wisdom on anyone; we do it to look like we're cool.

And yet, at the same time, adults should know that young people often set a goal of "out-cooling" their elders. There's a bar to be raised, which explains why outrageous antics seem to get more audacious as time passes. If you were drinking at sixteen, they have to do it at fifteen. If you had pictures passed around school, they'll get them posted online.

It's a game of generational one-up-manship, taken, ironically, to new lows.

Today's middle school student is exposed to stories from parents and other older folks, they're inundated with wild exploits of their peers online and on television, and they're left wondering: If I don't participate, am I out of the social circle? What's wrong with me?

You'll discover that a lot of this ties together. To balance out the negative images that get glorified, we could use some positive images to show the benefits of good behavior. And yet those are being dropped out of fear of alienating a few—see the earlier discussion on valedictorians and honor rolls.

What can you do? If you're someone who truly wants to help turn the tide, you might look at two things: (1) What are you glamorizing in the face of young people? and (2) Are you quick to reinforce positive images?

We've already mentioned the glamorizing of bad behavior. But what about the other side of that coin? You have a lot of influence in the attitude of students toward education.

I created a feature on our morning radio show called News For Nerds. In it, I mention a handful of the coolest scientific stories of the previous week, whether it was a new rover landing on Mars, or a study of why women like men who dance. The goal, however, is to talk about them in fun, conversational ways, including several people in the discussion, and mentioning things about the deepest science stories that actually have a helping of humor in them. In other words, I make science fun, without dumbing it down. It's nowhere near as difficult as you think; kids, by nature, *want* to learn. You just have to show them in language and images that they understand.

As a fundraiser for The Big Brain Club, we created shirts that say "Gettin' My Nerd On." The response has been huge, with requests from people (including kids) that I never would have guessed. It's a way of strutting about knowledge.

When I visit schools, my mission is to leave them with a feeling that it's not only okay to enjoy reading and writing and science and math, but it's cool. My radio background gives me a slight advantage when it comes to credibility with them, but instead of using that resume to hype the ridiculous exploits of music stars, I use it to gain the confidence and respect of kids in order to instill a new way of thinking about their education. Because I was a nerd at their age, it's almost like a cause-and-effect equation come to life before their eyes.

I dislike the term role model, but it does have somewhat of an effect in the dismantling of negative stereotypes. Let's talk about that.

## Discovering Brave Leaders

One of our challenges lies in the area of mentors, or what are often referred to as role models. I think it's easier to simply look upon them as examples.

As with most things, there are bad examples (of which, for this discussion, we could find a staggering number), and there are good examples. Where does one find good examples, the people who live and breathe the mission of The Big Brain Club?

Complicating the matter are a couple of factors that I often think about. One involves misdirection. In other words, you might be excited to have that famous actor or famous athlete or famous pop star come into the school to tell kids to focus on their education . . . but kids are kids. When they see Joe Sports Hero walk in, all they want to talk about—and think about—are the sports exploits. If Susie Pop Star came gliding in, complete with rock star outfit and dark shades, she might have every sincere intention of helping students to use their brains and to get an education, but c'mon! I mean, that's Susie Pop Star up there! Let's get her autograph!

It's not the fault of the kids, and it's not the fault of the celebrity. In fact, there's no fault at play here. It's simply human nature; we're sometimes easily distracted from a message by the messenger.

The other challenge with examples/role models/mentors is the potential for complete and total backlash, and it can come in two forms. First, you're using a celebrity who is going to have negative baggage, like it or not. The Big Brain Club might be a cause that people can rally behind, but if they personally don't care for a particular celebrity, or if that celebrity has done something in the past that might reflect poorly on the foundation, then the message is as tainted as the messenger.

For that matter, if you get pulled over for a speeding ticket (just to use a minor example), no one will know except you, and maybe your close circle of friends that you choose to tell. If our celebrity gets in trouble, the entire world knows immediately, thanks to social networking and the media's insatiable desire to report every single thing in the world of famous folks. The Big Brain Club is putting its own image on the line when it relies too heavily on celebrity endorsements.

Don't get me wrong: If celebrities want to tout the obvious benefits that this foundation creates, we would love their help. We're simply careful when it comes to aligning ourselves in any official capacity.

**And yet there are examples** that *do* get us very excited. I'm not convinced that the best role models are celebrities, or at least not the celebrities that usually spring to mind.

From the early days of the foundation, I've loved telling young people the true stories of "nerds" who have done the coolest stuff. Yes, we all know the stories of Bill Gates and Steve Jobs, and the countless other nerdy men and women who created tech empires. But I'm not thinking of just tech people. We like to profile people on our web site who have ultra-cool jobs, and who got those jobs— the jobs that young people would love—because of their intellect and their innate curiosity and ambition. Those are truly excellent role models. They make it clear that you can be cool and still use your brain, which is essentially the mission statement of The Big Brain Club.

There are numerous examples. When she was ten years old, Juliette Brindak co-founded a company called Miss O and Friends. Essentially her goal was to bridge the gap between girls who had "outgrown Barbie but are not ready for Britney." Now the company's CEO—and a very mature 21-year-old—Juliette oversees a web site that has grown into more than just a safe, age-appropriate spot for young girls to interact; it caught the attention of Fortune 500 giant Procter & Gamble, a primary investor in the business. Never mind that Juliette's net worth had reached $15 million by the age of nineteen; her site was also tabbed by *Inc. Magazine* as one of America's Coolest College Start-Ups, and she even has her own syndicated column (a sort of Dear Abby for young girls) that is featured in more than 700 newspapers.

And then there's Jacob Schindler. In the late 1990s Jacob was a sixth grade student in search of a school science project. That search led him to Mars. The inquisitive student gave some thought to the creation of a breathable atmosphere on the red planet, and wondered if the plant known as kudzu held the answer. Kudzu, originally from Asia, had migrated with people to the American continent in the 19th century, where it began to elbow native plants out of the way. It's something of a parasite, gobbling up more and more territory. Through his studies on the plant, Jacob stumbled across an environmentally friendly way of curbing kudzu's growth, thus saving millions of acres of native crops.

Jacob, in an interview with CNN in 2011, talked about his potential future in the world of botany. But he also said: "I've learned a lot of life skills: research, public speaking, making connections. It's opened a lot of doors for me. Otherwise, I would probably be home this sumer, just washing the truck."

Washing the truck, versus rolling up his sleeves and solving a massive problem in feeding the world's hungry.

Riley Carney is the author of a popular series of books for teens and tweens, *The Reign of the Elements* series. She's also founded a non-profit group called Breaking The Chain, which promotes literacy among some of the world's poorest nations. Her efforts have already led to the building of three schools in Africa, and the donation of more than 20,000 books to elementary schools.

Oh, and Riley is still a teenager. Wonder what she'll do once she hits twenty?

These are young adults who have excelled in their fields because they understood from an early age that just being cool in high school wasn't going to get them anywhere in life. It's a fun high for a couple of years, but—as with many highs—it leaves you flat and empty afterward. Compare that with publishing novels, building schools, developing a solution for feeding the hungry, and creating a helpful web connection for young girls to reach out in a safe environment.

Smart is Cool.

You don't need to be a parent or teacher in order to make a difference. All it takes is a student here or a student there to begin the cycle of positive influence. Young people can quickly learn that saving the world isn't limited to recycling and checking carbon emissions. Saving the world can also take the form of encouraging fellow young people to harness the collected energy of their brains, to take that magnificent computer within them and use it for good.

The positive role models for The Big Brain Club will need to involve the students themselves, and, as we saw with Juliette, Jacob, and Riley, they don't need to be celebrities. The challenge is getting one middle school student, then another, and then another, to see the effect that their influence has on another person. If enough students begin to accept their portion of responsibility for their own education, you'll see a difference. They'll begin to apply a collective, group power to the problem.

Adults have been trying for years. I'm willing to put some trust in the students themselves.

## Defining 'The Reward of the Challenge'

Let me appeal to your practical side. If we're going to take on something as important as education reform, we should at least understand what the students get out of it, as well as—believe it or not—what *we* get out of it.

Let's start with a movie, shall we? In the 1988 thriller *Die Hard,* Bruce Willis is trapped inside the massive building at Nakatomi Plaza, while a hardened group of bad guys are wreaking havoc just a few floors below him.

The police arrive, surround the building, and then haul in some giant spotlights to bathe the grounds in brilliant light. But the bad guys simply see easy targets, and proceed to bust out some windows and then shoot out the massive lights. The street-wise patrol officer quickly points out: "They're shooting at the lights!"

But of course, per Hollywood requirement, the deputy police chief—who must never be smarter than the patrol officer—takes a bit longer to catch on. You can see the exasperation on the patrol officer's face when the befuddled chief finally announces: "Hey! They're shooting at the lights!"

I felt the same exasperation when I read a story in *USA Today.* The headline stated: Low Standards Are a Hurdle to Graduation.

In essence, the article pointed out that researchers at Princeton University had made an astounding discovery: students, it seems, do better when challenged!

Hey everyone! They're shooting at the lights!

Yes, it took a research study to conclude that students excel when we stop coddling them and actually challenge them intellectually. Call me crazy, but I thought people learned *only* when challenged. It applies to every field, from the arts to sports to—yes—education.

I'll give you a real-life example. When I was a kid my dad was in the Air Force, and we usually moved every couple of years. During my third and fourth grade years we lived in Italy, which is a terrific cultural experience for any snot-nosed nine-year-old. We lived in town, near several other American families, but smack-dab in the center of Italian lifestyle. Our little group of elementary-aged Yanks would often take on the Italian kids in pick-up soccer games. Listen, we were raised on football and baseball, and had some cockiness in our blood. We could play *any* sport. Bring it on.

The Italian kids crushed us. Repeatedly.

But we never gave up. By the end of the second year, after getting our noses figuratively and literally bloodied for so long, we began to win a few times. Not always, but enough that we earned the respect of the locals who had generations of soccer greatness flowing in their veins. We took the challenge of going up against a stronger opponent and *we learned.*

Think about aspiring musicians. Now think about how rapidly they improve when they put in work with demanding instructors. I remember that we had one of those cheesy organs in our living room, the kind where you pushed a button and got a little samba rhythm, or another button brought you a waltz tempo, and another oozed a "rock beat" out of the speaker. (Trust me: it wasn't rock.)

But I never received formal lessons, and I never progressed beyond just plunking around on the thing. The musicians you know and love today spent hours and hours—and then more hours—practicing, honing their craft, and trying to master something difficult. If they'd stuck with *You Are My Sunshine* or *Chopsticks*, how many would have played Carnegie Hall?

Given all of that, why would anyone—including researchers— ever believe that education is any different? Lower the bar on educational standards, and you'll reap what you sow. Chalk it up as yet another casualty in the misguided movement to focus on self-esteem rather than education, often dumbing-down the lesson so it's not too difficult, and passing poorly performing students from grade to grade.

Lowering our expectations of students sounds suspiciously like the old joke about the guy who tells his doctor that it hurts when he moves his arm over his head. The doctor, of course, says, "Then don't move your arm over your head."

Too many people in our society are all about the shortcut, but educating our young people should *never* involve a quick-fix. Who in their right mind truly believes that the answer to our nation's eroding literacy rate is to make it *easier* for students to skate by? I've spoken with numerous sixth grade teachers who are pulling their hair out over the reading abilities of the students that they inherit in the fall. A mind-numbing number of them are reading at approximately a second or third grade level. And they've been ushered along in a system that forgives all and passes the problem on to someone else.

Lowered expectations are insidious, because they shuffle the responsibility down the road. Only, too often, the road has no end of the line, and the buck never stops anywhere until a young adult walks across the stage with a diploma that they can't read. If anything, our expectations—and educational demands—should be raised, beginning in early elementary school.

The Big Brain Club is not about every kid making the honor roll or getting a straight-A report card. It's about helping young people to feel proud of their intellectual achievements, and that happens when they actually achieve something. You're not too proud when you're stuck on *Chopsticks* throughout twelve years of school. When we get back to giving students (of all income levels, all races, and all walks of life) respect that is earned through achievement, I guarantee you they won't let you down.

In fact, I'm guessing that their performance will be lights out.

Let's look at it another way. If we know it's better for the student, then how is it better for *you* when they have to confront real challenges, rather than skating by?

Let's use another story, only this time it stars my friend Sarah.

Sarah is a hard-working young woman who balanced a full-time job while she studied for her CPA license. If you, or anyone you know, has gone through that process, you know how grueling it can be. Sarah spent hours and hours studying for each of the four major exams which are tackled within the course of a year.

I chatted with Sarah's husband, Jake, about all of this while we sat in the stands watching a baseball game. After listening to his description of her arduous, exhausting journey, we both chuckled and agreed on one thing: *that's* the person we want doing our taxes.

That cuts to the heart of the Reward of the Challenge, doesn't it? How does it affect not only the student, but society in general?

You'll see applications of this everywhere, although they're sadly neglected by the Self-Esteem Patrol. My daughter-in-law recently graduated from nursing school. Over the past two years I watched as she excused herself from social occasions so that she could dive into textbooks that appeared larger than all of the *Harry Potter* books combined. I watched her spend weeks following her graduation, buried in study prep for another formidable testing procedure, the nursing boards.

But here's the bottom line: *that's* the person I want attending to me when I'm rushed into the Emergency Room.

The rewards of a challenging education serve not only the student, whose knowledge grows exponentially, but society as a whole. I want to push every student, regardless of her chosen field, because it serves both her and me. No, it's not selfish; it's logical and practical. When it serves me, it serves you, too.

You have to wonder about anyone who subscribes to the 'make it easier on kids so they feel special' program. When the time comes for them to hire the accountant, or choose their doctor, will they suddenly demand an over-achiever? You can't have it both ways.

Academic achievement by an individual has a ripple effect on everyone else.

Think of how we demand excellence in almost every aspect of our lives. We want our telephones to work, we want the lights to come on when we throw the switch, we want the bank to handle our accounts perfectly, and we demand the aircraft be flawlessly designed and maintained. Well, you can't harvest excellence without cultivating it in school.

In this regard, the reward of the challenge is shared by all.

# CHAPTER 7

# THE BIGGEST OBSTACLES

I'm a practical guy, so when I begin a difficult project I like to consider what I'm up against, weigh the odds, explore the pitfalls, and reference several other cliches. It's important to know what to expect, because a movement such as The Big Brain Club is going against a virtual tidal wave of opposition, consisting of multiple elements:

 ✓ Fear of change or rejection
 ✓ Plaque
 ✓ Apathy
 ✓ The elementary factor

All of these lie within the realm of human nature, which means the program is fighting not just that tidal wave, but a riptide that threatens to force us continually downward, pushing us further and further beneath the swell. Ask anyone who has worked hard to succeed in the face of long-established mindsets, or who has taken on the task of actually changing deep-seated perceptions. It's easy to get discouraged and throw in the towel. The combination of resistance and discouragement can mean utter failure.

But no matter how tough it gets, I'm not giving up, and you shouldn't either. Instead, let's size up the obstacles, one at a time, in order to knock them down.

## Fear of change or rejection

The Big Brain Club asks young adults to hold up a stop sign to behavior that's gained momentum for decades, and they are, in a sense, overwhelmed by the idea. It's much easier to just float along on the currents, right? When you go to a water park, how many people do you see on their tubes, coasting along down the lazy river? And how many do you see on their feet, slugging their way against the rush of water and bodies? You might occasionally see one or two giving it a go, but not for long; not only are they going against the onrushing current, but the people carried along by that current push them back, sometimes violently.

It's tough to go against the crowd. Adults hate doing it, and for students it's only appealing to them if it gives them some sort of social cache. (See the earlier thoughts in Chapter 3 involving rebels.) And in this case, being a 'nerd'—at least in their eyes—isn't the social standing they desire.

Whisk yourself back in time, and recall your not-so-glorious days in middle school. Cliques were initiated left and right, coalescing before your eyes as like-minded kids grouped together. It wasn't too dissimilar from the birth of our solar system, where various particles of gas and dust swirled around and around the new star which had kicked on with a bang. Eventually corralled by gravitational attraction, these collections of debris formed individual planets, with their own squadrons of moons circling in awe.

Middle school students are the same way. They scatter across the campus until they are gravitationally drawn into a group, usually one that holds a specific attraction for them. This group will usually orbit one particular student, and we remember that kid, too: the one who was loud, assertive, and often manipulative. Once under the command of the group's mass, it's tough for a student to break away. In most cases, he *never* breaks away. It seems that once you're pigeon-holed into a social sphere, you're there for the duration. Woe is the poor student who dares to challenge the social strata of middle school or high school. It's not just a matter of bucking that one loud-mouth; you're going up against an entire group. Police officers have plenty of stories of young people who attempt to break away from a gang; that's an extreme example, of course, but the same herd mentality—and its pressure—applies.

As adults we might look back on it and wonder why we allowed ourselves to be swept along with a group of people who today hold absolutely no attraction for us. It's not much different from our reaction to seeing our yearbook picture: *What was I thinking?* But things are much different through the lens of time and experience. As a teen or pre-teen, you were simply caught up and lacked the wisdom to reflect on your choices. You made quick decisions based on gut reaction, flavored by the attitudes of the crowd.

This is a critical issue in the world of education. It's tough for a young person who truly wants to excel academically, and yet is socially tied to a peer group that doesn't share her educational values. She feels trapped, bound to an unspoken code. On one hand she wants to succeed in class, but she also longs for acceptance from the group. To push back against a group mentality that scoffs at education would—in her mind, at least—subject her to a student's version of excommunication. She would stand out for all of the wrong reasons.

Going against the grain of academic attitudes is tantamount to a social taboo. If everyone in the group believes that intellectual success brands you as a dork, then it's much easier to just go along. In the teenage world, current social status far outweighs future benefits, which are nearly impossible to envision and seem so far away.

If you want to deconstruct this just a bit more, factor in the notion of *whose side are you on?* Remember, educators and parents—representing authority and the man!—are in favor of you doing your homework and hitting the books. If you take that side as a student, aren't you selling out? Aren't you siding with *them*? That alone will subconsciously give a seventh-grader second thoughts. He'll almost feel as if he's being a traitor to his kind.

On our radio show we've joked about how a young person will wait to see how her parents feel about an issue before choosing her own position. It often seems to happen when it comes to a boyfriend/girlfriend situation. As one parent told me, "As soon as she found out that her father and I really liked this boy, she completely lost interest in him."

Frustrating? Certainly. But let's not pretend that this particular behavior is exclusive to the current generation. Those of you with a sly smile on your face right now probably were that same kid, asserting your independence in any small way that you could.

All of this contributes to the power of the tribe, and it manifests in a variety of ways to subvert a student's desire to achieve. It plays on a primal human fear: being alone or outnumbered against a sizable foe.

## Plaque

I'm not talking about your teeth or your arteries in this instance, but we might as well use them as an example.

Any dentist will tell you that regular cleanings are beneficial because they allow the hygienist to remove the damaging layers of gunk that build up on your teeth. If unchecked over time, plaque will allow bacteria to secrete substances that actually tear down your tooth enamel, creating cavities and often leading to gum disease. But when we're lazy and think, "Oh, I'll worry about that tomorrow," we often find that it's too late.

Poor eating habits may contribute to a plaque buildup in our body's arteries, which can restrict blood flow, or break off and lead to clots which eventually can cause heart attacks. It's easy enough to ignore the warnings plastered all over our daily lives, and continue to abuse our bodies because we don't see the actual damage until it's too late.

One of the reasons The Big Brain Club has its hands full is because of the layers of plaque that have built up over the decades in terms of negative stereotypes. Where once the smart kid on campus was revered and honored, she's now largely forgotten or ignored—unless a few scamps choose to embarrass her with snide remarks and cruel nicknames. And this has been going on for so long that now the filmy residue of ignorance has grown into a thick tartar of stupidity. The longer we let it fester, the harder it will become to scrape it away.

Consequently, the longer we wait, the more difficult it becomes to recruit champions who are bold enough to charge in and take on the challenge of smashing the negative image. Ten years of plaque is tough enough to chip away; thirty years is practically concrete.

Intellectual plaque also creates a false sense of normalcy. After years of accepting the stereotype of the socially-inept smart kid, it's hard for young people to comprehend that it even *could* be any other way. In their minds they might not even recognize this as a challenge because . . . well, because it's *supposed* to be this way, isn't it? The sun comes up in the morning, the Cubs won't win the World Series, and smart kids are nerds and dorks. Society established the playbook, and entire generations followed it, executing the roles in the only light in which they've seen them. Tearing up that playbook is difficult on both an individual level and a societal level.

Compounding the problem of this perceived normalcy is the very real issue of a generation that is numb to accomplishment.

When the Apollo program placed twelve men on the moon in the span of four years—using technology that today is dwarfed by the portable device in your pocket—the world sat in stunned amazement. Businesses shut down as the world focused their attention and their respect upon a handful of humans who had done the unfathomable. The pioneering feats served not only as a testament to human ingenuity and determination, but they also brought together people from around the world, inspiring hundreds of millions. These miracles of science provided a legion of young people with the idea that they could accomplish almost anything, and instantly our world changed.

But look what's happened in the succeeding years. We've witnessed one astounding achievement after another, to the point where today nothing fazes us. The pace of technological growth has moved at such a dizzying pace that we've grown completely numb to what once would have stopped us in our tracks. We're not just spoiled by the possibilities at our fingertips, we're impatient if they don't improve overnight. Today's phenomenal scientific feats—some that have gone far beyond the moon, and are unfolding billions of miles away, *on the surface of other worlds*—are relegated to the tiny postscript of a newscast or an afterthought on a web site . . . if that.

Think about that for just a moment. As you read these words, electronic representatives from our little blue planet are sniffing and analyzing the atmosphere of Mars, while another majestic creation has already plummeted to the surface of Saturn's mysterious orange moon, Titan, taking pictures of a landscape that includes mountains, valleys, lakes, and river beds. Each of these vehicles left Earth about one hundred years after the Wright brothers first demonstrated human flight. That's within one human lifetime, from the beaches of North Carolina to an alien world a billion miles away.

How many people can even name the craft cruising through Saturn's system? Can you?

The ability of our achievements to impress us and, more importantly, to *motivate* us, has waned. Where Neil Armstrong and Company once ignited a desire to learn and to explore—both inner and outer space—we've now been subjected to a form of mental Novocaine. We're numb to spectacular feats of engineering and growth. We expect them. And we definitely take them for granted.

This numbness only adds to the plaque that continues to build, and makes it more and more difficult for young minds to appreciate their opportunities.

In a sense, it becomes a preacher/choir situation. The Big Brain Club promotes a message that is enthusiastically embraced by individuals and organizations who get it, while those who could most benefit from it are isolated in a world that doesn't recognize that a problem even exists.

I've spoken at conferences of educators who nod throughout my presentation. I've had librarians and teachers who cheer the foundation's mission statement, and who offer to help in any way they can. Countless parents have reached out with thanks, often with stories that parallel Dylan's (see the Introduction), and who encourage me to spread the word to others. They all get it. They've either witnessed the heartbreak of children dumbing down and forfeiting a promising future, or they're in the trenches right now, battling against a perception which handcuffs their attempts to make a better life for young people. They've seen firsthand what the foundation is fighting for, and they endorse it wholeheartedly.

But that plaque is a thick shell insulating the people who most need to hear the message. It repels standard efforts to break through. It has created its own defense system, and often seems impervious to penetration. On multiple occasions, when I've finished speaking to a packed auditorium of middle school students, teachers or principals will walk up to shake my hand and say pretty much the same thing: "It's good for the kids to hear this from someone else, because it has more of an impact coming from someone outside the school."

In other words, the students *expect* to hear the message from their teachers and they've almost developed a mental barrier to it.

Or it has become the white noise that lies at the lower limits of their hearing, and it doesn't register coming from a traditional educational authority figure. But when it's delivered by someone in the real world—someone who, in their minds, doesn't have the same agenda as their teachers—it suddenly reinforces what those teachers have been telling them. Now they have a practical application for a message that they've heard but either have ignored or missed altogether.

Preaching to the choir. If you're holding this book or ebook in your hands, or listening to the audio version or a podcast, then in some respects you're already on board. You recognize that a problem exists. The next step is to build a concerted effort to dissolve the years and years of plaque buildup, to rally a generation to see things not only as they are, but as they could be.

## Apathy

It's not enough to read about the problem and nod; it's up to us and succeeding generations to become part of the solution. As with many difficult challenges, however, we fight a disappointing element of human nature: apathy.

The word evolved from the Greek *apatheia*, which describes an absence of feeling. In our modern sense we use it to describe an indifference, often brought about through a feeling of helplessness.

That seems about right in this context.

Back in the day, correct spelling and proper grammar were not only encouraged, but expected. It was rare to find a mistake in a newspaper or magazine article, and correspondence—whether between individuals or within companies—was meticulously accurate. In a way, it was a matter of pride.

Today? Read your email. Read the online posts. Read the sign boards outside of businesses as you drive past. Read anything. Chances are that you'll encounter error after error after error. Ten minutes before writing this paragraph, I read a post on a social media page from someone who misspelled four of the seven words in their sentence.

And nobody seems to care. We're not only rapidly sliding down into an illiterate well, we don't seem to be bothered by it whatsoever. I used to chuckle when I saw someone mistakenly describe another person as a "looser," when they meant "loser." Oh, the irony. Today, however, it would seem that there are more people who misspell the word than get it right. We have, sadly, become a nation of loosers.

Many people have their own pet peeves: *There/they're/their* and *your/you're* are near the top of the list, while others wonder why it's so hard for people to spell *weird*. The examples are endless.

But the issue isn't simply the mistakes. What's most troubling is that there seems to be no sense of shame, and certainly no rush to correct or even improve the situation. Americans, to a large extent, are apathetic to their accelerating illiteracy. Pride is reserved merely for how people see themselves in the mirror, not in how they present themselves intellectually.

I make mistakes. I'm not always perfect grammatically, and I'll sometimes misspell a word in an embarrassing situation (for ages I somehow could not grasp the second "m" in *accommodate*, just as I disrespected the second "r" in *occurrence*). The difference, however, is that I *wanted* to correctly spell the words.

Today there seems to be a stubborn insistence on misspelling. There's little incentive to improve, and I've often wondered what that's about. When I've asked, I've heard answers such as "I've always spelled it like that," or—this is the worst—"So what? You know what I'm talking about."

I think what you're talking about is an apathetic attitude toward education and learning. Why bother, right? Who cares if it's spelled correctly? What difference does it make?

C'mon, let's watch *Jersey Shore*.

Perhaps most troubling is the suggestion that you're somehow a snob or an elitist if you even broach the subject. I've seen blog posts that receive critical remarks in the comments section regarding the author's poor grammar and/or spelling . . . and the unfortunate soul who pointed out the errors is ferociously attacked by others. What message should we take from that? Well, in America today, the sin is not in committing a rash of spelling mistakes; no, the crime is in pointing it out or attempting to help. That makes you a snob.

Better to be the kindest illiterate nation in history.

Somehow, somewhere, pride has to involve more than just that image in the mirror. Smirking over a dumbed-down lifestyle might seem cool at age fifteen or eighteen, but by age thirty it borders on pathetic. At age forty and above it's downright sad.

And yet, fighting apathy in any situation is an uphill battle. Not only are the forces against you, but charging headlong into that battle can get you derided as a zealot. You'll hear things like "Chill, man," or "Why are you so worried about it?"

I've tried to imagine what the world will look like in forty or fifty years. Today there's still a pretty good chance that a resume chock full of mistakes will automatically eliminate you from consideration for a critical job. Not to be too cynical, but what happens when the people responsible for hiring that critical person can't spot the errors, or, even worse, are apathetic to them? Does that lead to a society that will never correct its course?

How important to us is it? I understand that language has evolved over the centuries, but it would be a cop-out to compare the Middle Ages' access to information with the mind-numbing amount of data—and educational opportunities—at our disposal today. This is not a natural evolution; it's dumbing down.

We are, unfortunately, often a lazy nation when it comes to intellectual accomplishment. It's too easy to ignore the problem, and allow it to snowball until illiteracy is the norm. Restoring a sense of intellectual pride in succeeding generations is decidedly a challenge for The Big Brain Club.

## The Elementary Factor

This is an interesting facet in the battle against childhood intellectual peer pressure because it involves the parents' inability to envision the future. No, not their own; they seem to have no problem with that (see Chapter 3). It's when their children are involved that they become myopic.

I encounter this most frequently when I speak to a large group of parents. Invariably someone will raise their hand and announce, "I don't see this as an issue at all. My son is doing very well in school, and none of this has come up."

The young person in question is often an elementary school student, so I'm not surprised.

It's difficult for a parent to imagine their child going off the rails. Young Ashley or Adam is enthusiastic about learning, and they consistently bring home glowing reports from elementary school. At bedtime you can't seem to read to them enough, because they're sponges when it comes to their favorite books; they can listen to them over and over again. And, when they begin to read for themselves, they often find a favorite author or series and tear through the entire set.

At times like these, parents not only are blind to the inevitable pressures, they're practically militant in their refusal to believe. What we're dealing with in this situation is a parent who goes into defensive mode, because essentially what we're doing—in their mind—is calling into question their ability to raise a child. How dare we insinuate that their child will become 'one of those kids'! Preposterous!

The Big Brain Club's message is not an indictment against parenting abilities. It's a warning bell of what often happens when that young person leaves the nest for the difficult world of middle school. Years of proper upbringing in a strong home, one that's rooted in a deep-seated belief in education, provides a remarkably strong base for a student's path through school . . . but it's hardly a shield. Story after story, each from a parent who felt their child was immune from peer pressure following a sparkling trip through elementary school, reinforces the point.

Take David. He was in the audience during one of my presentations and sought me out afterward to shake my hand. His story is consistent with so many others.

"My daughter is now twenty-one," he said. "In elementary school she had perfect grades, and loved everything about school. She loved to read, to write, she enjoyed math and science. It couldn't be better.

"Then, as soon as she went to middle school, things began to change. She fell in with a crowd of kids who weren't the best role models, especially regarding education. At one point I discovered a series of notes that she had exchanged with some of these friends, and I noticed a little code at the bottom. It said: GGGGG."

David told me that he wasn't sure how to approach his daughter about this, but eventually he confronted her with questions about her new attitudes surrounding school. And he demanded to know what GGGGG stood for.

His daughter chuckled and said, "Good girls get good grades."

I must have raised my eyebrows at this point in his story, because he nodded. "Yeah," he told me. "Good girls get good grades. And that is *not* complimentary; they mean it in the most sarcastic manner possible. In other words, if you get good grades, then you must be a good girl, and nobody wants to be considered a good girl. Good girls are goody-two-shoes, they're ridiculed, and they're shunned. So the last thing you want to do is get good grades. It puts you in *that* camp."

The GGGGG footnote was a way for this clique to remind each member that in order to be considered part of the cool group, you have to blow off your studies. Whatever you do, don't get caught being a good girl.

Just two years earlier, David might very well have been one of those parents in the back of the room at my presentation, his arms securely folded in front of his chest, shaking his head, and muttering, "Not *my* daughter."

Dylan's parents, who we met earlier, were likely the same way, and were eventually just as stunned as David. It's the elementary factor, the inability of parents of primary school students to comprehend exactly how powerful the forces of peer pressure become once their gifted student walks the halls of middle school and high school.

There are schools in America that are aware of the damning effects of intellectual peer pressure, and they do a brilliant job of minimizing it, often creating a culture where young people are insulated from the most heinous examples. Parents affiliated with these schools tend to also be skeptical of any problem, because, again, they don't see it. Their children are fortunate to be cocooned within an educational environment that promotes learning and literacy.

The irony is that their experience creates another layer of apathy, an attitude of "if it doesn't affect *my* child, then it doesn't exist."

It does exist, and it's crippling the chances of millions of young people in America to get that necessary head start. It's costing them an opportunity that they too often take for granted, one that many children around the world beg for.

Convincing parents of a second-grader that their daughter will, in just a matter of a few years, be on the verge of ditching her school books and cutting class—while at the same time ridiculing the students who keep their heads down and plow forward with their studies—is a tough assignment. They perceive it as an insult to them and to their children, which prevents them from understanding the issue at its core. David put it very succinctly: "Once a parent sees what happens in middle school, it opens their eyes. The best you can do is alert them to the problem, and hope that they recognize the signs early."

**I'm thrilled to know that the issues of intellectual peer pressure,** of intentionally dumbing down, don't apply to every child in America. Unfortunately that good news creates a false impression that all is well within every school. Sadly, it's not.

# HORIZON MIDDLE SCHOOL

**What's the intangible component** that determines whether or not a struggling school is able to turn things around and get students to dedicate themselves to academic excellence? In the words of one extraordinary principal, "It takes a sense of trust."

Nestled within an older and economically diverse neighborhood in Aurora, Colorado, Horizon Middle School was floundering in 2007 when Dr. Jeanette Patterson took the reins. There were few workable systems in place, discipline was abysmal, and morale—including that of teachers, students, and parents—was low. "Teachers and students had given up," Dr. Patterson said.

I sat with her and media specialist Sarah Pauly to discuss the effects of this climate on a school's ultimate scorecard: academic achievement. Horizon certainly isn't the only school in America forced to fix issues that go far beyond reading and writing, and I was curious to find out how these educators went about repairing the underlying damage in order to energize an atmosphere of learning.

While many people tend to think of schools as sterile factories that pump out course work and assessment tests, in reality there's an almost palpable feel in the hallways, as each school exudes its own personality or character. That aura can influence attitudes toward learning; schools that reek of despair or indifference often see a correspondingly bleak outcome in test scores and graduation rates. When the faculty and the students give up, it's game over.

The first step in creating a climate of success begins at the very top.

Dr. Patterson immediately spoke of trust, and in fact referenced that word many times during our interview. "One factor in developing trust within our school was our Positive Behavior Support program," she told me. "We begin with our school mission, in which we say the path to respect is SOLE: Self, Others, Learning, and Environment. Students who exhibit outstanding traits in each of these areas are rewarded with Paws (the school's mascot is the Husky), and because of this they feel a sense of purpose and self."

The Paws at Horizon are marked with a specific accomplishment, such as respecting others, helping out the faculty, going above and beyond on a project or assignment, and giving back to the community.

Additionally, the school regularly hosts community nights, gatherings that include not only the teachers and students, but the parents as well. It's not unusual to see a game of dodgeball between the adults and the kids, or a spirited basketball game. Within a year, Dr. Patterson began to see a sense of community within the walls of their campus. It wasn't long before that spirit spilled outward, and students were volunteering to help deliver food to homeless shelters.

Horizon had never really developed an active Student Council, but that changed, too. Also, Pride Day would find the student body walking the halls in their school colors, blue and white. Unless she's away on business, the principal is out in front of the school each and every morning, greeting students as they arrive, and then back in the same spot every afternoon to say goodbye and to thank them for a good day. After the first bell rings at 8:05, there's five minutes of music that streams through the halls and classrooms. One week it might be R&B, another week country, or something specially requested. It provides an energetic start to each day. Oh, and don't be surprised to find Dr. Patterson dancing in the halls.

**All of this sounds terrific,** but don't be fooled into thinking that all of these warm touches are for aesthetics alone. There are demonstrable differences that are a direct result, and they're the kind of differences that parents and communities are clamoring for around the country.

Four years ago Horizon Middle School was in the doldrums academically. Today, the students are staying in school (attendance has surpassed the 97 percent mark), and there's a distinct air of accomplishment down every hallway. When I speak at schools I often mention at the outset that, along with all of my accomplishments, I'm a nerd at heart. This is generally received with a rolling of eyes.

At Horizon, when I revealed this bit of information, there's was a thundering round of applause. Close to one thousand students cheering academic achievement. Cheering.

Troubled students at public schools often face what's called a referral. This is where a faculty member will connect a student with a therapist or other professional in order to facilitate an understanding—and, they hope, to reach a satisfactory outcome—of an individual child's issues. In 2007 Horizon Middle School charted 1600 referrals. By 2010, after three years of their SOLE mission and its subsequent changes, that number was cut in half. Dr. Patterson says that for 2011 the total would likely drop further still, to about 650. That's a sixty percent decrease in behavioral incidents in forty-eight months.

Students are finding ways to involve themselves outside of traditional classroom activities. The technology director at Horizon takes on student helpers who proceed to build computers at home on their own, and also roll up their sleeves to tackle the random tech problems that pop up around the school.

Each year the administration interviews students who would like to become The Voice of Horizon. These students are tapped to read the morning announcements, lead the school in the Pledge of Allegiance, and recite the school's mission statement.

**But what is it about this middle school's culture** that has made a difference in the actual academic successes? I perked up when Dr. Patterson mentioned the future.

One of the primary goals of my foundation, The Big Brain Club, is to encourage young adults to see their future. Yes, how they perform today in the classroom is important, but understanding *why* they're doing this work is a vital ingredient. Left on their own, most pre-teens and teenagers won't look down the road and envision their destination. They're too caught up in today.

Hammering the concept of consequences, both good and bad, makes a world of difference when a seventh-grader is sitting in class. It can't be just lip service; a concerted effort must be made to help that student visualize what their education will mean when they're twenty, when they're thirty, and beyond. When they begin to truly understand why they're in school, their attitude changes. It's no longer about just getting through another day of tedious homework; it's suddenly about providing the kind of tomorrow that they want.

At Horizon Middle School they hold a series of assemblies with one purpose in mind: See the future.

"At the beginning of the school year we have an Expectation Assembly," said Dr. Patterson. "I talk to the students about finding the diamonds in the sky."

Finding the diamonds in the sky. I love the poetry of that phrase, but more importantly I love what it signifies. Before they get down to work for the year, these students are being prepped for success later in life, with specific discussions about attitude, approach, and achievement.

Before long these are no longer your typical middle school students. They are encouraged to participate in an online community known as College In Colorado, a site that prepares young people by focusing on career and educational opportunities. To enhance that strategy, Horizon students are invited to hop on a bus and head up to the University of Colorado in Boulder, where they tour the campus and then afterward attend a CU football game.

Remember, these are middle school students. Stop one in the hallway and there's a good chance they'll be able to tell you what college they're interested in, and what career path is most interesting to them right now. Sarah Pauly smiled as she said it adds a sense of expectation in not only the students, but in their parents. The adults are thrilled to see their kids excited about education to the point that they're already planning their futures.

**In four years,** this one school in a middle class suburb of Denver—a school that is evenly split between white children and children of color, a school that has about forty-five percent of its students on free or reduced lunch programs— completely turned itself around. What once was a school of despondent teachers, students, and parents has become a model program that embraces its young scholars, teaches them to respect themselves and each other, instills a real, committed sense of community, and challenges each student to plan for her future.

Problems that once existed within the school walls allowed the education program itself to fall through the cracks and get lost. Today when a student leaves Horizon Middle School they arrive at their next stop in a better place than most. "They show up for high school prepared," said Dr. Patterson. "They're happy, and they're excited. They're ready to go."

Administrators at the nearby high schools agree. They call Horizon's principal and tell her that the kids she's sending over are "risk takers." In other words, they don't sit back in class with their arms crossed; they excel.

These are young people who have not only seen their future, but enthusiastically embrace it. They understand that taking their education seriously is one of the keys to a happy and successful life, and they're not ashamed to proudly say so.

They cheer nerds. And they find the diamonds in the sky.

# CHAPTER 8

# THE POWER
# OF POTENTIAL

A s we've seen, there are concerns, certainly, and obstacles that require a methodical, concerted effort to overcome if we're going to turn around the decline in academic achievement. But there are reasons to be optimistic as well, because there's another side to the ledger; it's where you'll find the power of potential.

That potential is embodied within educators and parents. And, although it's often lost in the glare of pop culture's glorification of the intellectually lazy, it can be found within society at large, too. But perhaps the best news of all is that the solutions also lie within the hearts and minds of America's younger generations. While cynics scoff, I steadfastly believe in the determination of students to implement positive changes to not only their own personal destinies, but also to the outcome of their generation, as well. Of the three primary factors that inspire confidence in the mission of The Big Brain Club, young adults provide the anchor.

✓ The collective power of parents and educators
✓ Pockets of success
✓ A generation determined to succeed

**The best strategy for success** will involve a combination of all three, and to be honest we can—and should—be motivated by one particular blunt assessment: The alternative to fixing the problem is to spiral ever downward, until we're left with a nation whose intellectual spark isn't strong enough to sustain it. Film director and screenwriter Garson Kanin said it quite well: "I want everybody to be smart. As smart as they can be. A world of ignorant people is too dangerous to live in."

His vision of a world of ignorant people brings to mind the dystopian darkness of futuristic novels. That prospect is frightening enough to motivate many of us to act. Fortunately there's a shelf life on cool ignorance; where Americans draw the line depends on just how much they're willing to sacrifice. I'm guessing it won't be much. This will need to be a come-from-behind victory, but the seeds are there, resonating in the power of the potential.

## The collective power of parents and educators

The first time I took The Big Brain Club's mission for a test drive was in 2004, when I spoke at what's known as a continuation ceremony for a Denver-area elementary school. The sixth grade class was finishing their year, preparing to move on to the hectic world of middle school. They perched politely to one side in the school's cafeteria, while the parents, grandparents, and assorted family members and friends sat in the audience.

I spoke for about twenty minutes, detailing what they were about to encounter in the coming years, and describing the specific challenges awaiting them in middle school. I'm guessing that the majority of speakers at these ceremonies dwell on the past, congratulating the kids on a job well done, and reliving some of their favorite memories of elementary school. But I kept the focus on their future, encouraging them to keep their eyes on the goal, and empowering them to choose long-term academic excellence over a temporary pursuit of coolness.

I went so far as to describe the tactics that others would use to bring them down. You could've heard a pin drop in that room, and the students were laser-focused on me without one disruption or one quiet whisper to a neighbor.

It was an unscripted presentation. I looked upon it as a rehearsal of sorts for the eventual Big Brain Club mantra, but I was fired up and curious to see what the reaction would be, not just from the sixth graders, but from the adults present in the room.

I was floored. As soon as the assembly ended, the kids began their celebration, excited about the upcoming summer break and their new status as middle schoolers. Many of them came over to visit with me, and to thank me for speaking the truth. It was my first indication that I'd touched a nerve.

But when I turned to my right, I saw a long line forming in front of me. The parents, family members, and school faculty began to shake my hand and talk about my presentation. I heard the same comments over and over again:

> *Thank you for talking to them about this.*
> *You are dead-on with your message.*
> *This will make a difference, you watch.*
> *It's about time they heard this from someone*
>     *besides their teachers.*
> *You need to get the word out.*

**It was a stunning endorsement,** and one that I began to hear repeatedly. Parents of middle school students are thrilled to see an organization that champions education beyond a basic book drive, while teachers and librarians are happy that someone outside the traditional school system is willing to roll up his sleeves and help tackle the problems. For years schools have unfortunately been treated as dumping grounds by some parents who expect the classroom teacher not only to educate their child, but to practically raise them.

Wendy, a sixth grade teacher said, "The philosophy behind The Big Brain Club is exactly what we try to teach, promote, and reinforce every day." I believe her. I also believe that she, and her fellow educators, get little to no help from outside their ranks.

Following that initial trial run in 2004, my school presentations gradually morphed. Where before they were purely writing workshops and assemblies, they now incorporated elements of The Big Brain Club and its message, helping students to prepare for the jungle of middle school and high school life.

I speak at education conventions, too. Each year I address meetings of librarians and school media specialists, with gatherings that cover every region of the country, a variety of district sizes, and a broad range of socioeconomic levels. By the end of each conference I have a stack of cards from schools that want to either bring me in to address the students, or arrange for an online video conference.

For years teachers and school administrators have been squarely in the nation's crosshairs over declining test scores and literacy rates. But it's shortsighted to believe that we suddenly have a dearth of qualified teachers, or to believe that somehow overnight our classroom standards have disappeared. The reason educators are fired up about the mission of The Big Brain Club is because they understand how students' attitudes toward education play a vital role in the process; when that ingredient is fouled, the entire dish is ruined. For once there's a program in place that involves students as part of the solution, rather than demanding that teachers do more with less . . . again. They've heard countless suggestions from many factions, including those from posturing politicians, but rarely have they heard *tangible* solutions. The Big Brain Club resonates with them because it's a candid evaluation that incorporates blunt, honest solutions.

And perhaps, just as important, we've reached the point where not only are we alarmed at the results of student assessments, but our backs are against the proverbial wall in terms of funding. Cuts are devastating many school districts around the nation, while programs are being pared down or eliminated altogether. Between the sobering academic results and the grim financial picture, educators and parents are faced with an ultimatum: We have to do *something*.

Human nature teaches us that people will often let societal problems slide without addressing them, right up until the point where it personally affects them. Well, now we have educators losing their jobs while vital school programs are slashed, at the same time that parents and the general public are being asked to pony up, either through increased taxes or through endless fundraising requests (coupon books, candy bars, magazines, flowers, and frozen breakfast pastries). Both sides—the educators and the parents—have a personal, vested interest in getting results *now*, not ten years from now.

And it's not as if the product of this push is something we're dispassionate about. We're talking about our children and their future; parents want the best for their kids, and teachers come to think of these students as "their kids" in a matter of weeks. In other words, we're motivated. Yes, we all agree that we want to preserve the planet, and we want to protect our pets, and we want to end malaria worldwide. But as soon as our kids are in trouble, we rally like never before.

The key is the *collective* power of parents and educators. There are instances when these two sides butt heads because of the emotional nature of their respective relationships with the students. Parents may sometimes question the tactics used in the classroom, and teachers may be justified in their frustration at the lack of parental involvement. Those issues aren't disappearing (unfortunately), but in order for the mission of The Big Brain Club to get a foothold, it's time to marshall the forces. We all have a common goal and an opportunity to make a difference.

This collective power, with a determination to correct the problems we face within the education system, plays an important role in turning things around. If only a handful of adults bought in,

I'd fold up my tent and go home. But the support is overwhelming, and the will is there.

## Pockets of success

In an earlier Snapshot I detailed the students at Horizon Middle School, cheering the acknowledgment of nerd power.

Now add the renewed marriage between brains and brawn.

One of the many challenges facing education in America is the perceived barrier between athletics and academics. I say *perceived* because it doesn't have to be that way. But sadly, generations of young Americans have drifted through their school years believing that they had to choose one or the other.

However, one of the most powerful tools in creating a successful school program involves melding those two cultures, fusing the emotional, adrenaline-based athletic forces of the school with the enthusiastic, achievement-oriented system of academics. Packaged together, and taught to empower each other through support and encouragement—a key element to eventual success—a school can recognize significant gains while generating a self-replicating model of educational power.

In short, a school that not only emphasizes athletics and academics, but creates a culture where both sides appreciate the other, is a winner on the field and in the classroom. This culture of compatibility also creates an intangible dynamic: community pride. Show me a school that excels in both arenas, and I'll show you a school that is a vibrant source of pride for any town.

A case in point: Preston Middle School, in Fort Collins, Colorado. I visited with the principal, Scott Nielsen, and the school's media specialist, Tracey Winey, and what I heard inspired me.

Preston started strong when it originally opened its doors in 2004, but within a couple of years enrollment began to drop. More and more parents were opting to transfer their children to a different school in the area, one that they believed provided a stronger emphasis on academics, particularly math and science. Preston, it seems, had developed a reputation as an athletically dominant program, but not one in which classroom excellence was stressed. Enrollment plummeted, and by 2008 it stood at less than 700 students.

Scott was in the unique position of having experienced life on both sides. Initially a teacher at Preston, he moved briefly to their rival school before being hired back at Preston. Once he assumed the helm, he sat down with the faculty and laid out his vision for the future. Tracey Winey recalled that not everyone was on board at first.

"Don't get me wrong, we're proud of our athletic success at Preston," she said. "But Scott wanted to emphasize academic excellence as well."

Boy, have they. During a presentation at Preston in early 2011, I stood at a podium in their gym, facing almost one thousand students, faculty, and parents, with a backdrop that was inspiring. Lining the walls of the gym are the signs you expect to see at most schools: Championship banners in various sports, along with state and regional finals acknowledgements.

But upon further examination, I was thrilled to spot an assortment of other banners right alongside these. State math champions. Science awards. Even banners that proudly displayed the school's big wins in the state robotics tournaments. At one point, I was informed, of the 40 students in the entire state who qualified for this fascinating science tournament, seven of them hailed from Preston.

Basketball champs and science champs. At this school they get equal time and equal acclaim. And, according to Nielsen, the results have been spectacular. Not only has it instilled a sense of unity and bonding throughout the student body, but enrollment has skyrocketed. Parents who previously found reasons to pull their students out and pack them off to neighboring schools suddenly returned in droves. Preston became one of the most respected—and honored—middle schools in the state of Colorado, and enrollment swelled to almost 900.

Scott, Tracey, the school's faculty, and the student body have embraced the concept of The Big Brain Club, and won't be deterred. In mid-2011 Preston was named a finalist—and ultimately a winner—in the Schools of Distinction Awards, an annual program sponsored by the Intel Corporation. Eighteen schools across the nation were tapped as outstanding examples of academic institutions that are preparing tomorrow's leaders through their innovative math and science programs. That certainly describes this comeback story in Fort Collins.

**The pockets of success** aren't found solely on traditional campuses. Many parents who home-school their children have reached out to applaud the efforts of The Big Brain Club, and in so doing have clarified one of the reasons for choosing their path. As one mother told me in an email:

> *"The peer pressure to dumb down is the primary reason we moved (child) from public school. No knock on the teachers; it's the atmosphere of the kids themselves that brought her grades down from straight A's to mostly C's and D's. Once out of that environment, she again began testing above grade level, and is excited about going to college in two years. More people need to hear your message."*

But the answer needn't reside only outside the public school system. Consider this comment from a middle school counselor.

> *"Once we recognized the problem of dumbing down and noticed its destructive effect on impressionable students, we countered by personally thanking and rewarding those who stood up to its attack. Getting some of the older students to take*

*on a leadership role in the school was our quiet way of breaking the chain of abuse."*

**Breaking the chain.** It's a terrific metaphor for how teachers and parents can halt the infection of negative intellectual peer pressure from spreading. Think about it; if a sixth grader begins middle school with an enthusiastic outlook toward education, but is taunted by fellow students—often older students—he's much more likely to reciprocate as he progresses through the grades. For him, it's almost as if he's been taught "this is how it's done." Kids learn from their peers, both the good and the bad.

So when adults are able to break that cycle, as this counselor explained, and allow enthusiastic learners to move upward from grade to grade without a poisonous attitude toward education in the air, they lessen the chance that succeeding generations will face the pressure to dumb down. By eliminating some of the destructive links in the chain, counselors and dedicated teachers are allowing students to focus on their studies without fear of intellectual bullying.

I love hearing the success stories that pour in from classrooms around the country. Creative minds certainly exist in education, including Wendy Kopp and her Teach For America program, as well as Dave Levin and Mike Feinberg, founders of the KIPP (Knowledge is Power Program) schools that began by targeting some of the most challenging school districts in the nation. The resources might be economically tight, but, creatively speaking, they are positively inspiring.

What Wendy, Dave, and Mike have in common is a vision that begins with the dynamic potential we find tucked inside every young mind. They've created systems and specialized programs that bring out the best in their students, and they won't be hampered by outdated formats and institutions. I would encourage you to find their stories, in books and online, to see just a handful of examples of how systems definitely can improve.

The best news of all is that success often breeds success. People are noticing the results of Teach For America's alumni, as well as the significant gains that are accumulating in KIPP schools. The Big Brain Club salutes their successes, and encourages every parent and educator to back the programs that do more than offer lip service and standardized tests.

## A generation determined to succeed

Cynics might proclaim that the younger generation is too spoiled, that they don't appreciate what they have, or that they expect everything to be handed to them. And while that may be true in some cases, I'm convinced that this is perhaps the most savvy generation yet. It's simply that their focus has shifted from education to socializing (boy, do they socialize!) in ways we could never have imagined. But let's not condemn them so quickly. Look in the mirror, my friend; if years ago *our* generation had been blessed with access to the tools that students have today, we would have been all over them, too. Yes, you would've lived on Facebook, iTunes, and YouTube as a teen (you likely do as an adult), so it's hard to fault today's young people for it.

There's a different way to look at this, however. A generation that expects the best of everything, and often runs at a clip much faster than we can comprehend, is also a generation that will *demand* the best. It's certainly not a matter of students not being bright enough to do the work; most adults are simply convinced that the drive is lacking.

Again, I'll disagree. Motivation never seems to be an issue with the young people I encounter. If anything, they might be a touch more amped up than in generations past. No, their drive is fine; the problem lies with the focus. If you're patiently waiting for them to get off the couch and help clean out the garage, their motor couldn't run any slower. Tell them that there's a party tonight at their friend's house, and they move at light-speed.

Now apply those dynamics to school. You'll discover that the *perception* of education is what today's students have to overcome before they can take real strides toward productivity. In a perfect world they'd fly out of bed in the morning, raring to go, ready to sprint to the classroom to begin soaking up the knowledge. But unfortunately they have some work to do before they get to that point. The first order of business is to mitigate the negative stereotype of academic success, to get them past the point where they worry about how they'll be judged by their peers. Essentially it's adding a step in their progress, a step that we shouldn't have to add . . . but we do.

On the surface it seems a nearly impossible task. For starters, how do you spread the idea amongst millions of students? Sure, one school, maybe even one town, can grasp the concept and make immediate and demonstrable improvements. This very chapter touched on pockets of success, and the various anecdotes included throughout the book suggest that change is happening on a small scale. But an entire nation?

Ah, remember that today's student is a master of socializing. In this case, it works in their favor when they take the concept of *Smart Is Cool* and make it viral.

Back in the day, a movement like The Big Brain Club would have relied upon a marketing campaign to accomplish its mission. It would've required posters, radio and television announcements, maybe even direct mail in order to get the word out. That was the only way you could spread a message with any kind of speed.

I don't think that kind of campaign is even in the best interests of this movement, so no tears lost over the so-called good ol' days.

No, the best way to spread this feeling among young people is to let them discover its truths for themselves, allow them to absorb and appreciate the benefits of the mindset, and then let *them* spread the word. What they can accomplish virally is mind-boggling. I watched two high school freshmen girls experiment with a popular social networking site. They created a fictitious new student, and imbued her with some pretty interesting characteristics. They casually mentioned something about this fascinating student to one or two people, and then quietly sat back. In just one day the imaginary girl had nearly 400 "friends," and was the talk of two entire schools. It took only twenty-four hours for hundreds of young people to voluntarily disseminate something (in this case some*one*) deemed noteworthy.

Twenty-first century students make up perhaps the best propaganda delivery system in the world, and that's not always a bad thing. Sure, sometimes it can be as shallow as the "popular new girl in town," but when they become evangelists for a cause, it develops legs. No, make that *wings*; it flies. The best delivery method for an attitude adjustment isn't through advertising; it's through word of mouth and a positive form of peer pressure.

Let me repeat that: A *positive* pressure.

I've had this discussion with more than a few teachers, and they seem to be of one mind. Peer pressure, although generally perceived as a negative, can sometimes turn the other direction. Just as young people have endured decades of pressure to dumb down, it's entirely possible that a new generation of students can exert pressure on their peers to pick up their game. And once the movement takes hold, the potential for viral efficiency can only help.

We're talking about a generation raised to believe that they can accomplish anything, and statistics allegedly show that their confidence level is higher than in any other country in the world. Yes, that's dangerous if they blindly believe in outcomes without doing the work to make it happen. But it also can be a catalyst in turning things around. If they were failing *and* felt like miserable failures, we'd be in even bigger trouble.

Young people are not ignorant of the stats. They hear about how they underperform when compared to many other countries; they see the test scores; they *know* when they can't do the work. But up until now it's been okay, because someone would be there to pick them up. As more adult factions implode over the divisive issue of education, it's not out of the realm of possibility that a cluster of motivated students will step up and take matters into their own hands. I pay attention during my school visits, and I'm convinced that the tide may begin to turn. The nucleus of the movement exists in some of the brightest and most outgoing teenagers in the world, as if they're poised for change. The trigger may be as simple as having a few leaders step forward.

If the negative peer pressure is spearheaded by a select few of the underachieving crowd, the rebound effect will be fueled by a select few students brave enough to lead the charge. Those kids cheering in the gym at the very mention of nerd-power carry hope. I believe that many young adults across the country are watching over their shoulder to see if someone—anyone—will publicly choose the smart route. They're looking for leaders to let them know it's okay to be smart and cool.

Once that happens, it will spread, and today's technological advancements make that not only possible, but lightning fast. A movement inspired by The Big Brain Club can capture the imagination of the world's most dynamic and—yes, let's say it again—confident students. When they get the green light to throw off the cloak of ignorance, they'll respond.

I think they're tired of playing dumb.

# CHAPTER 9

# THE EDUCATION
# TO-DO LIST

If you haven't guessed yet, I'm a passionate advocate for learning. To me there are few things more depressing than the notion of a bright, outgoing young adult throwing away his education and—with it—his best chance for a successful future.

The obvious question that follows is: So what do we do?

In order to change the educational landscape, and to implement the ideas put forward by The Big Brain Club and other concerned groups, we need to reach into the minds and the souls of today's younger generation. Simply standing on a soapbox and lecturing them to read and do their homework won't get it done, obviously. Instead it will take a concerted effort to communicate a message that stresses each student's personal outcome.

The payoff would be immense.

For a moment, imagine a society where students not only harness the staggering tools available from a technological standpoint, but fuel it all with an enthusiastic thirst for knowledge and growth. It's all right there in front of them, if they can overcome the toxic attitudes that drag them down. What if? What if, instead of a handful of students giving their best in the classroom, the *majority* of kids went all in? What if there was a sense of productive competition in the academic arena that matched what we see on the athletic fields?

What if pride in their education drove young people to go farther, faster, creating a world that took steps to eradicate disease, poverty, and hunger?

Grandiose visions, to be sure. But if we're going to begin to take those steps, programs like The Big Brain Club have to impact the educational system immediately. We're on a dangerous and slippery slope, and action is required right now. Here's what that action should consist of:

- ✓ Remind young adults that Smart Is Cool
- ✓ Teach students to see the future
- ✓ Redefine the idea of Role Models

**From the very beginning,** The Big Brain Club has emphasized that it's all about creating a generation of young people who are the very best versions of themselves. Once a student pulls herself up from the forces that are holding her back, she'll instinctively perform better in the classroom. That, in turn, will put her on a path toward contribution instead of reliance.

There are dozens of organizations that strive to help young people feel better about themselves. Touting self-esteem has become quite trendy in the last few years. I'm supportive of these programs as long as their goals are achieved through honest and valuable work on the part of the young person. Artificial esteem crumbles; earned esteem is lasting.

It starts with one simple equation.

## Remind young adults that Smart Is Cool

**We've been on a funny trip** the past few years. Back in the day, you were ridiculed for behaving in a dumb manner. Hey, they weren't known as 'blonde jokes,' but rather '*dumb* blonde jokes.' (And no, we don't encourage them; it's just to make a point.)

On television shows in the 60s and 70s, the buffoon was not someone to be idolized. Goldie Hawn was adorable on *Laugh In,* but no one aspired to *be* her.

Now, fast forward. How many young girls today would happily trade places with Lindsay Lohan, or Snookie? Neither has displayed overwhelming intellectual attributes, and yet they're considered pop culture icons. Our country has not only accepted dumb behavior, it has slowly come to associate it with what's trendy and—sad to say—cool.

I've had several in-depth discussions on this topic over the years, and in one of those chats a different spin was floated. Perhaps, a parent told me, our country simply ignores the stupidity. We know they're dumb, in other words, but we simply don't care. It's much too important that we emulate their lifestyle, and if that means dumbing ourselves down, then so be it.

The biggest problem with this thinking lies in the odds. How many stars and starlets hit it big in any given year? How many become rich and famous? Maybe twenty? Thirty? Should we be generous and say fifty? I understand that it's all relative, but work with me here.

Assume that as many as fifty young people become what we might consider rich and famous. Hold on to that number.

Now think about this. There are more than 75 million kids in school in America, from kindergarten through graduate school. 75 million. That makes the odds of a young person hitting it big as a star *less* than one in a million, and probably more like one in two to three million. In other words, it's not going to happen. The only thing that will provide for a young person is what lies between their ears.

And yet few people want to share that message. Instead, we're a nation obsessed with pop culture and the corresponding phony lifestyle. Phony because it's not a lifestyle that you nor I—nor anyone we know (probably)—will ever lead. It's an illusion, a fantasy created through the media. It's been with us for decades, true, but in the last few years it has become a glittering prize rather than an enjoyable distraction. It's no longer considered purely entertainment; instead it has become a challenge for young people.

It's simple: If the mindless movie star behaves badly and dumbs down for the masses, then that must be the way to success and riches. Dumb must be cool.

I'm not out to wreck anyone's dream of stardom. If your child has the talent and the drive, then power to them. But I'm not sure we need a nation of 300 million film and movie stars. Success is much more likely to come via education (mixed with that same drive) than through celebrity. The truth is, Smart Is Cool. Using their minds and developing their capacity for creative thought is the best chance that young people have in this world.

Based upon that assumption, it becomes a matter of offering an alternative to the glorification of manufactured celebrities. What is it that we can do to transfer the spotlight to the actual process of learning, and to the students themselves?

One answer is creating programs and curricula that highlight the inherent coolness that already exists in education. There are few people doing a better job of this than Steve Spangler, a former teacher who today works with educators and school districts, training teachers on how to make science—and, in general, learning—more fun. He's a frequent guest on the *Ellen Show* on television, where he uses ordinary, everyday items to create fun—and funny—experiments.

But it's not about just getting a laugh; it's about gaining real understanding of how the universe around us really operates. Teachers learn that by making science interesting, students are much more likely to retain the actual information. Spangler is the epitome of a program where Smart Is Cool.

My own foundation, The Big Brain Club, approaches students with two very different, but very effective, methods for incorporating a hip factor. For one, we provide schools with the technology necessary to reach 21st century learners. I'm a firm believer in connecting a young person's educational environment with what they see in the "real world." For years many schools—and, let's be honest, parents—resisted allowing society's latest gadgets into the classroom because it somehow, in their minds, bastardized the educational process. "Leave those toys at home," was how some people phrased it.

Really? Have you seen what some of these toys can do? And, more importantly, have you seen how well they can enhance the learning experience?

While some may squawk that "pen and paper were good enough for me," all it takes is a quick tour of schools that have implemented astounding new educational tech tools in order to recognize the benefits. The Big Brain Club provides devices such as SMART Boards, iPads, and other electronic tablets and gear. Why? Two important reasons: They provide an unprecedented ability to access and use information, and—this is key—they connect a young person's class-room, as well as her learning experience, with the world as it really exists around her. Rather than isolating a teenager in a cocoon of yesterday's technology and asking her to take her education seriously, we're propelling her into the advanced tech age with her education as a vehicle.

It's a key component to the Smart Is Cool campaign, and schools are embracing the manner in which the right tech devices can reach a heretofore unreachable student.

Next, the foundation works with schools to publish the creative writing of students. I'm continually impressed by the creative output of young people when they're encouraged to explore and to experiment. Essays, poetry, short fiction, journaling; the work that we've published is a testament to the latent talents that are percolating inside young Americans. For years they've assumed that they had to wait in order to express these creative ideas; when they're given the green light, the results are outstanding.

We've unveiled these professionally published books at school assemblies, and it's a moving experience. Parents approach afterwards with tears streaming down their faces, while the students are beaming. They are officially published authors, and the accomplishment makes them celebrities on campus. They embody the spirit of Smart Is Cool, and it's not something they'll relinquish easily.

The payoff comes from building a long-lasting attitude of academic achievement that will serve the student—and society— for a long time to come.

## Teach students to see the future

One of the best ways to emphasize the benefits of academic achievement for a generation bent on having the best of everything is to teach them the fine art of visualization. In other words, get them to see the future.

In Chapter 3, I covered the ingredients that make up the root of the evil, and one of those involved a young person's inability to comprehend their future. They're so tightly focused on the here and now that they ignore the consequences of their actions. To your average middle school and high school student, tomorrow is something to worry about tomorrow; today, it's all about perceived image.

If we accept that this is true, then what's the solution? How does one go about getting a young person to look past the limitations of today without sounding . . . okay, I'll say it: without sounding *old*. You can almost visualize a fifteen-year-old chuckling and saying, "All right, Grandpa."

And quite honestly, that kind of perception might play a part in why many adults refrain from getting involved in the process. But at some point you have to suck it up and do what's best for the students.

Let me describe the approach I take when I'm addressing a few hundred students at an assembly. Rather than giving them yet another speech about how they need to buckle down and do the right thing, or how they're missing out on an opportunity to better themselves—things they've heard over and over again, until it sounds like the warble coming out of the mouth of Charlie Brown's teacher—I start by painting an accurate picture of their day-to-day life.

The accurate description of their world involves acknowledging the importance of their relationships. One glance at online social networks will confirm just how crucial friendships are to a young adult. They won't deny it; in fact, they'll eagerly concede that it's just about the most important thing in their lives.

Then we talk about how important it is for some people to mock education, to disrupt the educational process, and to get as many people to join them as possible. Students see this firsthand on a daily basis; when you describe it, they'll recognize it.

And then the bombshell. I break the news that, as important as these peer relationships are, as much work as they put into them, and as careful as they are to sometimes bend their own values in order to fit in with 'the crowd,' there's something they need to realize. The day they walk out of high school, and for the rest of their lives, the number of people who will care about how cool they were in school is . . . zero.

Zero.

Nobody cares. Not one adult cares how cool another adult was back in school. No one cares what clothes you wore, what music you listened to, or what circles you ran in.

Nobody.

And students sit there, with a surprised look on their faces. As basic as this truth is, no one has ever explained that to them. As I point out, they're putting so much importance into trying to please a small group of people, for a tiny little window of their lives—maybe three to five years—and yet chances are they'll never see those people again after they graduate. They will have sacrificed the next sixty years of their lives for a few, short years of being perceived as cool.

And when these students walk out of school, the only things that people will care about are: What do you *know*? What are your skills? What have you learned? What do you have that can benefit my business?

Oh, you sat in the back of the class and cut up with your friends? That's nice. I think I'll hire the woman over here who graduated with a 3.8 GPA.

Oh, you never read a book? Hmm, that's interesting. Good for you. But I think we'll give the position to the young man here who spelled everything correctly on his application, and who graduated in the top ten percent of his class.

Oh, you were . . . *cool* in school? Next.

Now we're truly talking consequences, and it's not in a preachy form. It's real life. And what allows me to have this conversation with wide-eyed eighth-graders is that I live a pretty good life, with a nice house, a nice car, lots of nice vacations, and front-row seats at all of the best concerts.

And I'm a nerd.

Yes, I know there were a couple of movies about nerds getting revenge, but this isn't Hollywood, and it's certainly not about getting a laugh. This is the real thing. Because young people today tend to feel more entitled than previous generations, it's staggering for them to find out that the day is coming where they will have to earn something. And when they discover that goofing off with their pals means a lifetime of working long, hard hours at a series of dreary jobs that they hate—and never getting within sniffing distance of front-row seats or any other aspect of the good life—they are suddenly sitting up. I'm speaking their language.

One of the more powerful messages to impact young people is the idea of options. Again, this is a concept that appeals to the innate selfish side of most students.

On the radio show, I challenged my co-workers to each choose one food, and one food only. Then for a week we would all live on that food, and nothing else. Beverages were allowed (water, soda, juices, but nothing substantial like shakes or smoothies), but otherwise it was that one solitary food for breakfast, lunch, dinner, and all snacks. And no cheating.

One member of our show selected tacos. Another went with cheeseburgers. A third decided upon hot dogs (yes, hot dogs) and our traffic reporter opted for turkey sandwiches. I chose homemade pizza. The rules stated that you couldn't even vary the manner in which it was prepared; if you wanted a hot dog with mustard and relish, it would be mustard and relish each time. My homemade pizza had to carry the exact same toppings each time.

Why did we do this silly stunt? Well, I noticed that many times when people sat enjoying one of their favorite foods they would utter something along the lines of, "Wow, I love this. I could LIVE on this." And I wondered: *could* we really? What if we picked our favorite food and tried a social experiment to see if we really could live on it?

The listeners to our radio show immediately went crazy over the idea. We discovered that many listeners elected to try the experiment themselves, and their food choices were equally interesting. And what did we all learn? At the end of the week, it wasn't as if we were completely disgusted by our one food; we simply realized how much we missed the different options that we were used to. When you're suddenly confronted by the reality that your options have dried up, it's eye-opening.

It wasn't until later that I understood the strength of our experiment in relation to my work with students. It dawned on me that it was a perfect metaphor for the way in which young people often become hamstrung in their own choices.

Think about it: when people truly apply themselves in school and finish with high academic achievements, their options for a better life are vastly more significant than someone who barely sneaks by. Those with limited education have a handful of career choices from which to choose, and are more than likely the ones who will find themselves in what's known as the dead-end job. Their ability to maneuver into a more rewarding and better-paying career is hampered by the decisions they made long ago in middle school and high school.

We all want options. Look at the cereal aisle at the grocery store. You have a mindless number of options. Look at the app store online; it's a dizzying menu of options. Scroll through an online music store; you could never even begin to sample all of the choices at your fingertips.

Students who blow off their education severely limit their options in life. They're stuck with a few (not-so-attractive) choices. Those who knuckle down and do the work, those who push themselves, who aim higher and commit themselves to go farther, are rewarded with a plethora of options from which to choose when it comes time to make a career choice.

Instead of hot dogs for every meal, they'll be swamped with a feast of options.

**Listen, as I state repeatedly,** this message will not get through to every student. It's not possible. But there are students who take notice. There are young people who have everything it takes to achieve academic success; they've just never (if you'll pardon the pun) put two and two together. They've never understood that their actions today so directly and so significantly influence their tomorrow.

I love the writing of Ray Bradbury. In one of his landmark short stories, he put forth a remarkable vision of how the ripple effect of time can drastically alter the landscape of our future. His time-travel story *A Sound of Thunder* shows how one minuscule event—the killing of a tiny butterfly, millions of years ago—escalates through time until we're left with a future that is changed, and often not for the better.

The ripple effect applies in each young person's life, too. The choices that they make in the classroom today will have a cascading effect throughout time, and it's powerful to watch as this realization dawns on their faces in middle school. Until it's pointed out to them, using language that creates a visual comparison in their minds, they're likely to never imagine it for themselves.

## Redefine the idea of Role Models

The concept of role models is tricky. We're quick to apply the tag to individuals who have come nowhere close to earning it, other than the fact that they excel in some area in which young people pay attention. But, ultimately, we each personally decide what constitutes a role model; it might be a parent whom we look up to, or a teacher who made a difference.

What's important is that we recognize that young people will often cede their respect to someone we—as their elders—don't necessarily embrace. It might be a pop star, someone who is consistently blasted across the pop culture network, but often for the wrong reasons. Or it might be an athlete, one who scores regular headlines and *SportsCenter* highlight clips for their work on the field, but yet who lives a lifestyle that we disdain.

I have news for you: the pop stars and sports heroes that you admired were likely not much better.

Two things to emphasize here regarding so-called role models. For one, at some level even young adults recognize the difference between admiring someone's natural talents and embracing their lifestyle. I grew up idolizing John Lennon, but I eventually was able to separate his work as an artist and social commentator from his questionable lifestyle choices. Even John looked back later at many of those incidents and shook his head. As I matured, I was able to filter out the negatives, and instead use the staggering amount of Lennon's remarkable contributions to influence my own artistic and social efforts. Your kids will be able to do the same.

Secondly, one of the best gifts that an adult can bestow upon a young person is to help them to appreciate the differences between a person's shortcomings and their positive attributes. It doesn't have to be blatant; I've found that it's easy to draw a young adult into a conversation about one of their heroes, and to casually have them explain their fascination with the person. It's interesting to hear the way the student frames the choice, and often allows for a frank discussion about the good and the bad.

My parents both worried about my interest in John Lennon because their generation was quick to overlook his artistic side and instead focus on his drug use. But not once did they try to dissuade me from enjoying his work; instead, they gently inquired about what I saw in the Beatle, and talked about the poor choices that he'd made . . . without denigrating him as an artist. In my own quiet times, I know that I contrasted and compared the two sides.

On the flip side, I would never endorse picking your child's heroes for them. It doesn't work that way. Who are we to say what will inspire them? However, it *is* possible to bring attention to those who offer unique and positive alternatives to the usual pop culture stars. Many times it's someone that the young person might never have noticed on their own, someone who falls outside the traditional circle of celebrities, but who nonetheless offers an inspirational breath of fresh air.

In our various online postings for The Big Brain Club, we tend to avoid the term 'role model.' Instead, we include profiles of people who are making a difference in a cool way. Perhaps it's a young scientist who is making breakthroughs in an important field while also enjoying life as a rock climber. Or maybe it's the hot young recording artist who is graduating with honors and also helping other young people pursue promising academic futures. Or the movie star who graduated cum laude from an Ivy League school. Each of these profiles reveals a person who epitomizes the *Smart Is Cool* lifestyle.

I'm skeptical of what the media label a role model. In the first place, the word 'role' is important. If my son has no interest whatsoever in becoming a professional athlete, then it's hard for me to consider a football or basketball player as a role model for him. If he has no interest in pursuing a life in television or the movies, then the trouble-making sitcom star is not a role model. People in the spotlight might be of interest to many young people, but they play no tangible role whatsoever.

I've realized in life that my father and John Lennon were my role models. My father taught me responsibility and a strong work ethic; Lennon taught me to express myself and to try to help others through creative expression—with an emphasis on the creative. Each of these people played a role in molding the type of person that I became, each in unique ways.

As adults, it's important for us to recognize the potential power within people of influence in the lives of young people. We tend to overestimate the influence of pop culture's silly icons, and we miss the hidden forces of good within others who can truly inspire. It's incumbent upon us to reverse these extremes for the benefit of coming generations, and to redefine what the term 'role model' really means.

**These suggestions are by no means the only ways** of accomplishing our goal, and, indeed, there are many educators, businesses, and parents who already have found a knack for adjusting the focus of young people toward their education. On our web site, BigBrainClub.com, we have a blog that trumpets various success stories and the ingenious leaders who reach today's young people.

And yet none of these methods stand a chance of success without action, the subject of the final chapter.

# CHAPTER 10

# A CALL TO ARMS

Head nods are a good sign. When I speak to groups of parents, educators, and other concerned people, I see a lot of head nods. They translate to: *You're right,* and *I agree with you.*

And I appreciate that. I'm glad to know that I'm touching a nerve, and that I'm helping (in my own small way) students to become better versions of themselves.

But the next step is for you to join the battle. Just nodding and giving me a slap on the back won't get it done. And aren't we tired of platitudes from politicians about fixing education? *They* won't fix the problem; we—the parents, teachers, and students—have to be the ones to do it. Which might leave you asking: *What can I do?*

If you're serious about helping—if you're more than just a head-nodder—and you recognize how critical it is that we act right now, then you can definitely help. There will be countless opportunities for you, but let's focus on three strategies in particular.

✓ Stop glorifying bad behavior
✓ Prepare the canvas
✓ Be the best version of yourself

**I know that grass-roots movements** love to stress the importance of the individual, but in this case it's crucial. If you're in any kind of position of influence around a young adult, you hold more power than you think. *Making a difference* comes in many forms, which works out well since each person has their own comfort level when it comes to getting involved. As you'll see, your influence doesn't require much in the way of time. It's more about an attitude adjustment, really.

## Stop glorifying bad behavior

This can be broken down into a couple of categories: Other People, and You.

Earlier we touched on the fact that our country tends to make heroes out of rebels, but in the last few years it has gone way, way beyond that. To really grasp just how far it's gone, all you have to do is watch television: they've actually made a prime-time program out of the rehab exploits of celebrities.

Yes, many people will plop onto the couch at night, and spend valuable hours of their life fascinated by the drunken, drugged-out lives of 'stars.'

But that's just the beginning. There are dozens of shows that technically fall under the entertainment umbrella—and use the misnomer of reality TV—but which are in essence hour-long tributes to bad behavior, usually with B-level celebrities, or folks who are described as average people. Millions will tune in to find out just how outrageous they can be this week. Ugh.

Advertisers line up to sell their products on the shows, so the entire industry has been turned into a sad manipulation of ignorance for the sake of profit. I'm all for people making a living, but it's regrettable that it's generated through the glorification of stupidity. When one particular blond bad girl left rehab (again), companies lined up to shower her with jewelry, cars, and other gifts. They couched it in phrases such as, "We're congratulating her on her successful recovery." But it's a joke; it's a sleazy way of promoting their products by rewarding bad behavior.

Personally, I'd like to see these companies reach out and reward young adult celebrities who *don't* continually get arrested and/or sent to rehab. How uplifting it would be if we congratulated *them* for a lifetime of good choices. At the risk of sounding cheesy, I think that would send a message of encouragement to tens of millions of teenagers who teeter every day on the point of a decision regarding their own behavior.

Breathless reporters scramble to sensationalize each and every news report of a famous person who behaves poorly. So-and-so was arrested again for drunk driving; so-and-so was kicked out of this establishment; so-and-so is featured this week in an online video acting up in public; so-and-so . . . well, it's endless. It's yet another industry that is built upon glorifying bad behavior.

Two points here. First, don't believe for a moment that celebrities (and I cringe to even use that word) don't know exactly what they're doing. They are convinced that, in order to be perceived as outrageous and cool, they can't go more than a few weeks without topping the last stunt. They milk it, they revel in it, and they're convinced that it helps them to develop a reputation for being bad. Being bad is good business. It keeps them in the news when they're otherwise doing nothing whatsoever, and it spurs you to always remember their names. The poster child over the last couple of years is Charlie Sheen, who has laughed all the way to the bank. Oh yeah, he's cool.

Yawn.

Second point: I'm aware that it sells newspapers, magazines, and TV advertising because people *do* consume this fluff. I'm in the entertainment industry, hosting a top-rated morning radio show, and not a day goes by that we don't hear about some sad-sack celebrity who has gone off the rails, perhaps intentionally, in an attempt to manipulate their image and their press. But my industry is just as guilty of spreading the manure as the others.

I also don't expect it to go away. The cynic in me wonders just how outrageous the behavior can become, because in order to stay in the headlines you have to continually raise the bar. Personally, I've long since passed the point where I care. But it's here to stay, sadly. The question becomes how much of it *you* will personally support. And, more importantly, how much credibility you'll give it in front of young people who watch and learn from your own habits.

How we, as adults, receive this 'information' is important. Do you watch the reports with your middle-school student and chuckle? Do you say, 'Oh, my, Celebrity X has done it again!" In other words, are you giving the bad boy's continual bad behavior the attention that he's desperately angling for? Are you happily being manipulated, and, in turn, prepping an impressionable young mind to grow into a sheep as well?

I drove a friend and her two teenage daughters to the airport. When I asked if they had anything to read on the plane, the mom revealed a style magazine for herself, and then pointed at the magazines she'd purchased for her daughters to read. All four of the publications were "celebrity gossip" mags, such as *US Weekly*, *People*, etc.

There are countless reports about how parents pour sugar and fat into their kids' bodies, and we fervently raise a fist and claim that something must be done! Then we turn around and buy our teenage daughters *US Weekly*, the equivalent of sugar and fat for their brains. Sigh.

Young adults are sponges in so many ways, and one of those includes absorbing your fascination with drunken stars. And, honestly, is it *still* that interesting to you? Or has it just become routine?

**But we can't place all of the blame on celebrities.** They get too much credit, and too much blame, for many things in our daily lives, when the truth is it usually comes down to our own decision-making. It's just too easy to point the finger at someone else.

This is where the mirror test comes in. How willing are you to honestly evaluate your own craving for the bad-boy or bad-girl label? Let me give you some examples, and you think about it.

I have a friend (let's call him Dwayne) who is a smart guy. He works in a tough industry that's very competitive, he graduated with sparkling grades from a good school, and he makes a good living. He bought his first house at twenty-four, dresses well, and has never been in any serious trouble. I think he's had maybe two traffic tickets in his life, no accidents that were his fault, and certainly no arrests or other police issues. He's a sharp guy, with talent and a terrific work ethic. On top of that, he gives back to the community through some volunteer work and serves on the board of a non-profit organization.

And yet, whenever he's with a group of people, the only things Dwayne ever mentions are his 'bad boy' incidents: tales of getting too drunk to function, stories of pranks in college, elaborate details of the times he slept through tests, fights that he had in high school, hi-jinx that he's pulled in the office, the times where he's dabbled with drugs (although, I know, never seriously), and on and on.

If you didn't know him well, you'd be convinced that Dwayne was a hell-raising party boy, one step ahead of the law. Not once will he mention that he graduated near the top of his high school class; he'll never mention that he was on the Dean's List in college; he won't utter a word about his impeccable credentials in the business world, nor his time spent with the charitable group. Nope. Dwayne has completely bought into the notion that, in order to impress people, the *only* things you can mention are your 'bad boy' credentials.

You might want to suggest that Dwayne is merely being humble. But that's not it. It's one thing to not brag about your accomplishments; it's another thing entirely to brag about your missteps. It's a faux image, one predicated on the idea in America that good kids are dorks, and bad kids are the ones you want to hang with. As Dwayne illustrates, we know that good grades, good work ethics, and a good attitude are keys to a good life. And if that's the case, why are there so many Dwaynes out there? Why do so many good kids feel that they have to either dumb down or project an image of a bad boy/girl in order to be accepted?

I know other people exactly like Dwayne. At every function they crow about this infraction, or that brush with the law, or this time they were loaded, or that time they were high, or blah blah blah. I know these people; they're solid people with good jobs and good hearts. They might pretend that they're sheepish about their past, but it's an act. And they talk about it. All. The. Time. If you're truly sheepish about something, you *never* talk about it. No, it's not that they're embarrassed; they love the rebel image.

But remember our earlier point. When everyone is a rebel, nobody's a rebel. And the message that is repeated over and over in America is that being in trouble is cool, that it somehow bestows a badge of honor upon you and elevates you into some uber-cool club. But the club is a little crowded these days. Everyone, it seems, is trying to be a member.

And what's the cool club's response to the charge? Oh, Dom, you're such a goody-two-shoes. You're so square. C'mon, lighten up.

That's just it; I'm not a goody-two-shoes, and I have loads of events in my life that I'm not proud of. But you will rarely, if ever, hear me jabbering about them. It's boorish, in my opinion. I'm not interested in getting into a Coolest Contest with anyone.

I'm also aware of how this ongoing emphasis on bad behavior trickles down. When millions upon millions of young people witness it on a continual basis, what right do we have to demand that they do better? How in the world can we expect them to go to school and do the right thing when their parents, their uncles and aunts, their siblings, their neighbors, and everyone else spends countless hours laughing about the time they skipped class and got high? How do we expect kids to take education seriously when their closest role models love to go on and on about their wild-child exploits?

It's no coincidence that we see education really begin to tank in middle school. First and second graders aren't really paying attention to the rants of their elders; they're too busy playing games and reading their picture books. But seventh and eighth graders are listening and making mental notes. Cool behavior, as exhibited by the stories they hear, *must* be the way to go. Sadly, the examples they hear far too often are the wrong examples.

**If we're going to get the education ship headed in the right direction,** we need to look at what we hail as important in this country. If you want your kids to stay focused on making a better life for themselves, you need to make sure they understand what it takes to achieve that life. It doesn't mean lying about your past; it means placing the poor-choice incidents of your past in the proper context, rather than crowing about them.

It doesn't mean pretending to be a goody-two-shoes. It means realizing that the *good* things you do are worthy of a mention now and again, too.

It doesn't mean that you place your child in a bubble. It means exposing them to both the good and the bad, but framing each appropriately. Are you really that proud of getting drunk when you were underage? Are you really ashamed of making the Honor Roll? Are you really convinced that your friends will only respect you if you're a *bad boy*?

Think about it. There's a generation watching.

## Prepare the canvas

If you're an artist, you're likely familiar with gesso. If not, let me quickly tell you about it. Gesso is a chalk-based substance that artists use to prepare a surface for painting, usually canvas or wood. Left untreated, the acrylic or oil paint will have a difficult time sticking to the surface. Gesso coats the canvas and essentially gives the paint something to grab on to.

I look at books as the paint in the education community, while students are the canvas. Left untreated, those students will allow the books to slide right off of them, because unfortunately too many of their peers have announced that reading isn't cool. Educators roll up their sleeves and work hard to prepare lessons for crowded classrooms, but their efforts often don't stick. It isn't the teachers' lack of training, nor their enthusiasm; their students aren't ready to absorb the lesson. They're too often afraid that it will brand them a nerd or a dork, and they want to be accepted by their peers. The teachers are frustrated, and the headlines scream that we need to spend more money.

The problem is the canvas. It's untreated. Rather than spending more money on additional canvas, why don't we prepare the ones we have?

This is where you push the politicians aside, where you ignore the well-meaning (but misguided) fanatics who want to blow up the entire educational system, and where you assume responsibility through actions.

In what way do you interact with young adults? Are you a parent? An educator? A coach? A person in a position of influence in some other capacity, whether it's as a neighbor or friend? No matter what your role, you can make a positive impression upon a student.

Start by being aware of the issue, and then follow that by being aware of your own contribution to the problem or to the solution. I find myself engaging in an active dialogue with young people about the peer pressure they feel to dumb down, usually in group settings (through school assemblies or workshops), but also in one-on-one settings.

My own template for the discussion involves the steps it took for me to arrive at a good place in life, and none of it involved a silver spoon or any special treatment whatsoever. My life began in a lower-to-middle-class household, and until I was twenty-five I never made more than $17,000 a year. I worked hard to put myself in a position to succeed, first through education, and then with a strong work ethic. Nothing was ever handed to me.

What's your story? Are you confident and capable of sharing it with a young person who doesn't normally see adults as having once been kids? (That's a strange thought, but you'd be surprised how often it's true. We're merely adults, and in a kid's eyes we've *always* been adults.) Will you put aside the failed approach of trying to be a kid's best friend, and instead talk to them as a person whose responsibility is to show them the right way? Can you impress upon a young person the importance of their education and how it will serve them, not just tomorrow, but the day after tomorrow?

Do you read books and are there books and magazines around your house? How about reading the same book your child is reading, and then engaging in a conversation about it? It's a great way to make a connection with them, and you're emphasizing how fun and interesting it is to read.

The goal is to eliminate the negative connotation that many young people associate with reading, writing, and learning in general. It's critical that at the very least we create a learning environment that is open to the idea of academic achievement, rather than one that is suspicious of it. Our efforts are designed to erase the stereotypes of 'smart' kids, which have damaged the education movement of the past few decades.

It won't be an easy task. In a way, it's a lot like helping someone who's on a diet. If they fall off the wagon and binge one day on candy bars and cheeseburgers, it's imperative that they dig in their heels and commit to doing better the next day rather than just giving up. With the efforts of The Big Brain Club, we recognize that not every kid will be easy to convince, and we also know that there will be days when things look bleak. But this is an ongoing battle; we can't allow setbacks to discourage us, or to make us throw up our hands. Over time, we can create a healthy atmosphere for learning. And, like the dieter, it will become a lifestyle choice, rather than a temporary project.

Consider the young people in your sphere. They begin life as that blank canvas, open to almost anything. How you prepare that canvas ultimately helps to determine what sticks. Are you prepping it in a way that brings you pride?

## Be the best version of yourself

We ask a lot of the younger generation, and we fret over the direction in which they're heading. They're doing this wrong, and they're screwing that up, and they don't realize how good they have it.

Once again, let's break out the mirror. While it's easy to grade *them*, are *you* being the best version of yourself? So much about raising young people involves setting examples, and in the case of their education you might be tempted to think that it's out of your hands. You finished school long ago, right? But that thinking is wrong.

I understand that after twelve to sixteen years of school, many people are ready to leave it behind and get on with the rest of their life. But that's a sad waste of one of nature's most incredible inventions: the human brain. We have the capacity to keep learning, to keep growing throughout our lives, and yet countless millions of us shut down the learning center by the age of twenty.

Because you're officially out of school have you chosen to close your mind to bettering yourself intellectually? Instead of going into cruise control for the last fifty-plus years of your life, why not commit to an on-going infusion of education yourself? That doesn't mean enrolling in classes, or even taking online lessons. It's as simple as making a conscious decision to inject a bit of new knowledge into your life, in any form.

Examples? Here are a few.

I hear many people advocate for turning off the television, but I think there's a better alternative: change the channel. We like to believe that there are 500 channels but nothing on. In reality, there's an ever-increasing amount of viable, intelligent content awaiting, if you'd only get your mind out of the below-average terrain of most network sitcoms. The standard excuse for staring numbly at these brain-draining programs is: "I need a distraction after my long day." That's a cop-out, because distractions can come in a huge variety of ways.

Junk food satisfies you for the few minutes you're consuming it, and then takes its toll during the rest of your life. Well, a vast portion of television acts in an identical manner with your brain. The 'distraction' satisfies you for those thirty minutes, but you'll likely pay the price afterward.

You don't need to watch *NOVA* every time, and you don't need to completely eliminate your mindless escapism. But consider that the average home in America has a television on for almost seven hours a day. Seven hours! It adds up to a total of 250 billion hours every year. And, when asked, 49 percent of Americans even admit that they watch too much.

The stats regarding children and television viewing are too depressing to mention. But the microscope is on you, the adult, this time.

Becoming a better version of yourself includes becoming responsible for what amounts to at least 17 years of your life—the accumulated tonnage of TV viewing over an average lifetime. How much of that could be devoted to improving yourself in some way, through additional knowledge and information? What if even 20 percent of it was spent watching something informative, rather than 100 percent spent watching shows with manufactured laugh-tracks in the background?

**During a recent family vacation to Washington, D.C.,** I was once again blown away by the staggering amount of history and information packed into the national treasure known as The Smithsonian Institution. In three days I did my best to absorb as much as I possibly could, and still barely made a dent. But more importantly, I had a blast!

I'm a member of my local museum of nature and science, too, and every time I go I find myself in awe at the collection. The standing exhibits themselves are fascinating, but the traveling displays are usually incredible.

It's so easy for us to automatically default to the forms of entertainment that we've grown accustomed to: movies, television, or concerts. They're all viable options, and they're also convenient. You'll find movie theaters with a dozen or more screens just down the street, and there are multiple concert choices every week. But there's a special stimulation that comes from visiting museums and taking in the history and knowledge that so many people have worked hard to amass.

And, what's more, the diversity of the displays ensures that there's something for everyone. Egyptian mummies; space sciences; the animal kingdom; health sciences; and everyone's favorite: dinosaurs. You might think you know a lot about these things, but every visit to a museum reminds us of just how much we *don't* know.

Becoming the best version of yourself means taking pride in not only your community's museum, but taking pride in the expansion of your own knowledge.

**Get outside, and get involved.**

Sound funny? Perhaps. But these two simple suggestions allow you to explore your surroundings while also learning a bit more about yourself.

We tend to cocoon ourselves inside our homes, whether it's because we're tired after a long day, or because we've simply never considered the alternative. The physical activity alone will make you a better version of yourself, and maybe open your eyes to things you've never experienced.

Getting involved means becoming less selfish. Whether you volunteer in your community, become active in your school's PTO/PTA, or focus more time and energy working directly with your kids, getting involved is a chance for personal growth. Take it.

**If you're wondering why** a book about education includes a chapter aimed directly at adults, I'll give you two reasons. One, I think it's foolish for anyone to ever stop learning and growing. Who says that education is limited to kids?

And two, like it or not, young people are watching us and paying attention. We have a right to demand excellence from our young adult population, but this is a case where leading by example could pay big dividends. None of us should ever feel satisfied that we've learned all there is to learn. That way leads to stagnation and deterioration, both physically and in spirit.

I'd like to think that we, as adults, can set a good path for students to follow.

# CONCLUSION

I tip my cap to the hard-working people and organizations fighting the battles against peer pressure. There are countless groups who work to help young people overcome the peer pressure associated with drugs, with alcohol, with smoking, and with sex. All laudable efforts, and all of them facing challenges that seem to grow more difficult with each year. But without detracting from the work being done in these areas, I believe it's time to place an equal emphasis on another form of peer pressure that also can be crippling for a young person: Academic peer pressure.

The Big Brain Club is taking on what many consider to be the most important issue facing our country. We are, after all, placing our future into the hands of a generation that has more tools than we had, has more access to global information than we had, and is tied into a worldwide social web that we couldn't even imagine. Now it's up to us—and to them—to make sure they're ready to assume the reins.

Dumbing down is a recipe for disaster, and our student population is under enormous pressure to do so. And for what? To satisfy and befriend a malignant element of our society that values a perception of cool much more than they value academic integrity. We can't let that happen.

In closing, there are four important factors to keep in mind before you set this book down.

## We will never have a 100 percent success rate

Politicians and Pollyannas don't want to hear this. In their vision of a perfect world, every single student in America will get good grades, will go to college, will graduate, will get a terrific job, and will live a long, happy life. It's such a beautiful sentiment that I hate to be the one to snap my fingers in front of their faces, but a reality check is in order.

Not every student will get the message, and, sadly, many of those who do will reject it immediately. It's too easy to be bad (and too often rewarded), too easy to slack off in school, and too easy to take shortcuts.

The Big Brain Club is all about spreading the word and saving as many students as possible from making poor choices. My prediction is that we'll reach kids in each and every geographical and socio-economic section of the country. We'll wake up some students who have been manipulated by their peers and—sadly—let down by their elders. We'll successfully transform many young lives from what could have been a downward spiral into illiteracy and poverty, and help them to gain confidence and respect as they mature into productive, and intelligent, young adults.

But we won't save them all.

If we wait for the program that will rescue 100 percent of America's kids, we'll never, ever accomplish anything. Instead we need to present the truth about education and peer pressure, and help as many people as possible. The best thing we can do for students today is to help them to develop as many options as possible for their happily-ever-after.

## This message will be criticized for not being sensitive

Believe me, I've already heard it in some circles. The message contained in this book makes some people uncomfortable because it's not another volume on the bookshelves that simply teaches kids to feel good about themselves.

Kids will feel good about themselves when they have a reason to. *Artificial* self-esteem is a fraud that looks to capitalize on our good nature, essentially robbing us while daring us to deny that self-esteem is the number one issue affecting children. In my opinion, creating a false sense of pride—built on nothing but words—only undermines a student's long-term success.

My proposal is to give students the tools they need in order to actually achieve. Creating, producing, achieving, learning, and eventually contributing to society; *that's* where self-esteem is born in a young person. Individual pride is earned, something that is developed, not handed over. The idea of "teaching self-esteem" is ludicrous; while we're at it, why don't we teach kids to be taller?

The Big Brain Club strives to eliminate some of the nastiest barriers to a young person's education, which will go a much longer way in building their confidence than in hearing people continually gush over their ability to simply show up.

While I personally believe that environment does play a role in a child's education, it's not the only role. Part of that environment includes the attitude they encounter regarding their studies, and that's where I want to give them an assist. If they can learn to recognize the obstacles that hold them back, more students will push through these barriers and achieve success.

But I won't merely hold their hand and tell them to think happy thoughts. I'd rather get in the trenches with them and tell them about the real world. We can all get touchy-feely *after* they get a solid education. Until then, we have way too much work to do to stop and have a cupcake party everyday.

## Pop culture's poison is formidable

Proponents of The Big Brain Club will continually come up against the tidal forces of pop culture. And with the current cultural tide in the favor of dumbing down and being cool/rebellious, anyone who takes up this battle had better be prepared to be mocked.

The *pop* in pop culture is, after all, a shortened form of *popular*. And, as we've learned, the most important thing in the life of a middle school student is being popular, or, at the very least, being accepted by those who are popular. Pop culture both influences, and is influenced by, a surprisingly small core group of people. They determine what's hot, what's not, what's chic, what's boring, what's funny, what's in, and then the herd follows along. In order to get young people to reject the concept of dumbing down, you'll be essentially asking them to swim against the tide.

Our lifestyles today seem to revolve around empty calories, in many forms. There's the obvious example of junk food and 99-cent-value-menus—things that hook us not just with their low prices, but with their convenience. It's too easy for a hard-working parent to slip through the fast-food drive-thru after a long day at the office instead of spending another hour or so in the kitchen.

But our brains have slowly been trained to live on empty calories, too, in the form of pop culture's pre-packaged entertainment. And, just like many of the snack foods available today, these pop culture tidbits provide a temporary fix that, in the long run, supplies no beneficial value whatsoever. It's tough not only to wean someone from junk food, but from junk entertainment; once they're hooked, they almost know no other way.

For years I wondered how much longer the trends in music, movies, and other mass media would continue to slide toward the inane end of the scale, but I've come to accept that we might be at a point of no return. Instead of waiting for the national pop culture trends to change, we'll have to treat this as a grass roots effort that wins one small battle after another, and reaches one enthusiastic student after another.

## Young adults are so peer influenced that they'll wait to see how other students react to this message

When I visit middle school campuses, I can see several students immediately warm to the themes of The Big Brain Club. You can see on their faces that they're absorbing the information. They sit up to take in even more.

And then, in a flash, someone next to them will lean over, whisper something and laugh, and the spell is broken. In a flash, the student who showed interest, who was already beginning to plug themselves into the equation, is pulled back to the pack, like a vicious undertow in the surf. Sometimes they fight back and embrace the challenge; other times, unfortunately, they cave to the peer pressure. I might be speaking some special truth to them, but I'll be gone in an hour, while the slackers around them will be there day in, day out, constantly reinforcing their destructive lifestyle.

The answer may lie with smaller and smaller groups. When I speak to a gymnasium that's packed with 600 to 700 students, the party kings have a lot more sway. When it's a classroom of 30, it's much easier to keep their attention for a full hour. When it's a handful— or even one-on-one—it's exponentially more successful.

And yet, getting the message out to millions of students is time consuming; doing it 20 or 30 at a time might be more beneficial, but takes ten times longer in the scheme of things.

In a way, when I speak at an assembly I'm actually able to watch the process at work, up close and personal. I can talk about peer pressure, and immediately watch it materialize before my eyes, providing empirical evidence. I once joked with a school librarian that the slackers behaved like antibodies, attacking a virus that they subconsciously knew was invading their system. As soon as someone preached responsibility and academic integrity, they rose up to fight off the invader.

Educators have had to battle the problem of negative attitudes toward education, but anyone who takes up the charge of The Big Brain Club will see it come alive, too.

**These four factors** aren't meant to keep you from getting involved; they're merely intended to help you fight the good fight.

What's at stake? Well, our children's future, for one. But there's obviously more on the line. Like money.

In the 2010–2011 school year, public expenditures on elementary and secondary education in America were estimated at just over half-a-trillion dollars. That works out to almost $11,000 per child per year.

As of 2009 there were a little over 3.5 million teachers in our public school systems, the majority of them working harder than you could ever imagine. They get to school early, they stay late, they take a ridiculous amount of work home, they conduct student meetings, parent meetings, and after-school clubs. I laugh when I hear people point to a teacher's eight-week break in the summer and claim that they have it easy. Uh, try walking in their shoes for one semester and then report back about how easy they have it.

The Big Brain Club is convinced that we have the best teachers in the world. It's what they have to deal with that could really use an adjustment. I'd like to see them standing before a classroom of eager learners, not spinning their wheels before a room of posturing cool cats. When the students recognize what's at stake, I'm banking on the fact that they'll appreciate the material that's being taught, and embrace it more than they have. And that makes a teacher's job so much more manageable.

**The ultimate goal** of The Big Brain Club is to introduce young people to the benefits—and the joys—of *learning*. By extension, they often find ways to express themselves creatively, which brings another level of satisfaction and personal growth. Along the way they'll discover that they don't need to choose between being cool and using their brain; it's actually much more rewarding to do both.

In fact, it's more rewarding for all of us. Not only does it benefit individuals to roll up their sleeves and get involved, it's critical for the future of businesses. Sit down with any company's human resources manager and ask her about the crop of potential employee candidates that she's interviewed in the last year. She'll be the first to tell you—enthusiastically, I believe—that our focus should be on grooming the next generation of leaders, both in the world of business and culture. The product developed in our schools today affects each of us in the years to come.

Attitude is everything. When it comes to education, it's imperative that we shift the attitudes of students before we launch another national campaign to get kids to read more or to study harder. Until their minds are open—and they're willing to embrace a teacher's lesson—those campaigns are a hard sell, guilty of the cart-before-the-horse mentality.

If you're as enthusiastic as I am about The Big Brain Club and its mission, you have my thanks. If you're one of the very few people who take that enthusiasm and convert it into action, then you have my admiration. And if you're able to make a positive difference in the lives of young people through your determination, then **you're a hero.**

# ABOUT THE AUTHOR

**Dom Testa** is an author, speaker, and co-host of Denver's top-rated morning radio program. His *Galahad* series of young adult books has garnered multiple awards, including a Top Shelf selection by the American Library Association and an international grand prize from Writer's Digest.

He also is the founder and president of The Big Brain Club, a non-profit student-development foundation.

Dom lives in—and loves—Colorado.

DomTesta.com
@HeyDomTesta
Facebook.com/DomTesta

Since 2004 this 501(c)(3) non-profit foundation has been helping young people embrace the idea that Smart is Cool. Through a variety of free programs and services for schools, students, and teachers, The Big Brain Club has impacted thousands of students across the U.S.

The foundation's flagship Student Publishing Program has produced hundreds of first-time student authors in grades 6-12. Through generous individual and corporate donations, The Big Brain Club also provides a wide range of online and classroom resources, and delivers cutting-edge technology to schools.

BigBrainClub.com
@BigBrainClub
Facebook.com/BigBrainClub